WILLIAM TERRISS AND RICHARD PRINCE

Two Players in an Adelphi Melodrama

GEORGE ROWELL

THE SOCIETY FOR THEATRE RESEARCH
1987

First published 1987
by The Society for Theatre Research
77 Kinnerton Street, London SW1X 8ED

ISBN 0 85430 042 2

Printed in Great Britain at
The Bath Press, Avon

Introduction

The murder of William Terriss by Richard Prince was a fearful event grounded in dementia and baseless jealousy arising from another actor's cruel hoax. The assailant was unknown to his victim, and the murder, although not random, need never have happened. But the English popular stage had lost a valued and beloved actor, and in the closing days of 1897 and throughout the following half-decade, the crime was used by theatrical journalists to moralise in both favourable and disparaging terms about the profession, to sanctify the victim, and to excoriate Terriss's killer. The incident became a painful footnote to a decade which saw the first British performance of Ibsen and Shaw and the knighting of Irving. That decade, the 1890s, thus simultaneously marks the high tide of the Victorian stage and the advent of powerful new voices in the theatre, and – as a result of these voices – new audiences expressing different expectations for the stage. Martyred and beatified though he now was, Terriss and the "Adelphi melodrama" in which he had appeared were to be remembered as lurid anachronisms retained beyond their time. Equally did this stigma fall upon Lyceum and Her Majesty's plays and upon the Drury Lane "autumn drama", when offerings from these playhouses failed to reach the requisite high-seriousness or purposeful comedy increasingly in public demand. Not remarkably, theatre scholarship, stimulated by the changing ethos, celebrated the inward tide and condescendingly dismissed the outward flow.

In our rejoicing over "The New Drama" we have almost forgotten what an accomplished actor Terriss was and how his bluff persona, almost unaltering and unalterable in his stage roles and in his own private life, created the paradigmatic Victorian and Edwardian British Empire-builder: master of the unexpected, courageous and resourceful in adversity and danger, patriotic, chivalrous, puritanical but lightly sentimental, articulate and charming to females who, it was believed, were only just finding their tongues and discovering their self-sufficiency. (Their vote lay in the future.) In this study George Rowell suggests that British actors are judged in terms of their success or failure in Shakespearian roles. Such roles were not Terriss' *forte*, but Rowell now offers evidence that Terriss must be remembered equally as a significant performer and as an enjoyable idiosyncratic buoyant stage personality.

The Terriss persona was established through the vigorous Adelphi drama and its provincial equivalents. Adverse criticism of these plays is, in my view, both excessive and unfair. More than any drama of its time and as much as any other popular literature of the period, Adelphi melodrama described the current milieu. With some sociological accuracy and pictorial fidelity these dramas depicted social, economic, ethical, and (to some small extent) political problems facing their protagonists. Where such melodrama often failed was in ultimately turning away from these problems and instead resorting to conventional plot-formulae solutions. Terriss was a party to the worst and to the best of these practices. These melodramas, which regrettably, we too often judged through the fogged and inappropriate lens of Literary Criticism, embody a strong and recurrent emotional response to the exceptionally diffuse and contradictory experiences of the century: the growth and consolidation of Empire, industry, and urban centres with hitherto unmatched prosperity and comfort, but won at the exhorbitant price of colonialism, an exploitative factory system, and the many miseries and penalties of city life. The spectacle of William Terriss and Jessie Millward surmounting peril and adversity offered audiences optimistic confirmation that crisis, disorder, anomaly, and inconsistency were somehow reconcilable with stability and gain. Terriss, especially, was qualified for such melodramatic roles because of the duality of his signals to Adelphi audiences. In the midst of frenzied belief in the *mise en scène* and heroics of melodrama, he afforded the subversive chance to disbelieve, and, paradoxically, he offered belief to the sceptic and scoffer. Some spectators could believe, did believe, as a consequence of his easy panache, the message of melodrama that meaning and value and morality can be reimposed upon a world which has become chaotic. Other spectators caught in Terriss's splendid insouciance an irony inviting detachment, distancing, the enjoyment of clandestine mockery, and pessimistic reappraisal of Victoria's realms. This gifted actor held both visions in refined equilibrium. We, as scholars, must pay more regard to Adelphi melodramas as expressions of the fragmentation and incoherence of late-Victorian life and to Terriss as a performer adept at reconciling these contradictions. George Rowell's timely study, drawing on new material made available through the generosity of the Seymour Hicks family, is a necessary step in such reconsideration.

Members and scholarly friends of the Society for Theatre Research are well-accustomed to being grateful to George Rowell. He has thoughtfully explored much of nineteenth-century entertainment, carefully drawing a map which many of us confidently follow. Here we have another reason for gratitude. He looks again at the Terriss–Prince legend, cutting away the accretions of sentiment and deliberate red herrings, detailing the incident, exposing the reasons why this sad crime occurred. As such, fans of historical detection might read this book for its scholarly investigation of a byegone crime in a theatrical setting. However, students of theatre history will recognise more: that Mr. Rowell brings postpositivist historical analysis to his proven scholarship. This theatre history is not the study of great actors in great roles but an investigation of the close interworking of the provincial and London theatrical communities. The stars are there, but so too are stagehands and supernumeraries, their dependants and out-of-theatre companions, journalists, landladies, prostitutes and members of the audience whose recollections, strongly tinted with acknowledged bias, are admissible evidence. Audience expectations as much as current stage practice, both of these elements described and analysed by George Rowell, were the parameters that defined Terriss's success and proclaimed the extent of Prince's professional failure. We are encouraged to understand, even to sympathise with Terriss's killer (and we sense acutely what agony it was to live the futility and desperation of a supernumerary's life), not because Prince is admirable, but because his derangement was nourished in the same environment that made Terriss a star, an environment seductive to the outsider, but far less so to the professional, seasoning fugitive moments of glory and infrequent reward with hours of toil, meagre recompense, humiliation, and occasional brutality. It is indeed fortunate for us that the file on William Terriss's poignant death has been reopened because in establishing the facts of an event originally much misreported, we glimpse briefly but clearly into that environment.

David Mayer

Acknowledgements

I am delighted to have the opportunity of thanking two members of William Terriss's family, his granddaughter, Betty Seymour Hicks (Mrs. Spillane), and his great-grandson, Robert Stuart, for the encouragement they have given me while undertaking this study, and for their patience in awaiting its appearance.

An invitation from the Society for Theatre Research to lecture on Terriss was the starting-point of my investigation, and it is particularly fitting, therefore, that the work should appear under their imprint. I owe a special debt of gratitude to Dr. David Mayer for his valuable suggestions after reading the typescript, and for kindly providing the Introduction.

The difficulties inherent in reconstructing the ill-starred career of Richard Archer Prince were materially eased for me by the exertions of Mr. Angus Mackay.

Amongst others who have given their assistance I should like to mention: Mr. Henry Bristow; Mr. Alexander Clark; Professor Carl B. Cone; Professor James Ellis; Mr. Derek Forbes; Mr. Marius Goring; Professor Robert Lawrence; Mr. Jack Reading; Mrs. Nancy Sadek; Miss Mollie Sands; Mr. Donald Sinden; The Medical Director of Broadmoor Hospital; The Divisional Manager of the District and Piccadilly Lines, London Underground.

The Publications Sub-Committee of the Society for Theatre Research has been both patient and supportive throughout the preparation of the book, and I am especially grateful to its Chairman, Mr. George Speaight, and to his wife, Mary, who kindly provided the line-drawing of the Strand and its surrounding streets.

GEORGE ROWELL

Contents

Illustrations

I: The Setting

The heart of London's theatreland is usually recognised as Shaftesbury Avenue. This late Victorian thoroughfare, driven through Soho's slums from Piccadilly Circus to Cambridge Circus, acquired at the end of the last century a string of theatres: the old Shaftesbury, the Lyric, the Apollo, the Globe, the Queen's, the Palace. It also gained a reputation as the centre of West End entertainment which might have surprised the austere philanthropist, Antony Ashley Cooper, seventh Earl of Shaftesbury, after which the Avenue is named. Recent changes in theatrical management and the building of such prestigious playhouses as the National Theatre on the South Bank of the Thames and the Barbican Centre in the City have shifted London's centre of theatrical gravity, but the term "Shaftesbury Avenue" still survives as a label for commercial showmanship, popular programming, and a certain glossy style of acting and production.

To the Victorians themselves, however, the invitation to an evening's entertainment was aptly expressed in the words of the song: "Let's all go down the Strand". This historic highway, once a riverside track as its name indicates, grew in importance and changed in function over the centuries. From Mediaeval to Georgian times it boasted a series of palatial town-houses for the grand and powerful families of the nation. Princes of the Church built their London homes here: at various times the Archbishops of York, and the Bishops of Durham, Carlisle, Chester, Worcester, Norwich, Bath and Wells, Salisbury and Exeter all had their London residence in the Strand. Even longer is the tally of temporal

I

lords: starting with Simon de Montfort, Earl of Leicester, who built himself a stronghold on the site which later housed the Palace of the Savoy, most of the nation's leading families established a home in the Strand at some period. The names tell their own story: Northumberland, Mowbray, Howard, Arundel, Bedford, Essex, Suffolk, Buckingham – all had associations with the Strand and many have left a topographical legacy of some kind or other. As late as 1847 Disraeli could write: "The Strand is perhaps the finest street in Europe."

Nevertheless, by Disraeli's day the Strand was more closely associated with hoteliers and shopkeepers than statesmen or stately homes. The early years of the nineteenth century saw its development as a thoroughfare for trading and entertainment, and the building in 1817 of Waterloo Bridge opened it up to the fast-growing suburbs of the South Bank. Some of the accommodation it provided for visitors was exclusive and costly, notably the Hotel Cecil and from 1881 the prestigious Savoy Hotel, built by Richard D'Oyly Carte from the profits of his theatrical enterprise and as an adjunct to his brand-new Savoy Theatre. Other establishments were decidedly lowbrow, including the notorious "Coal Hole" tavern in Fountain Court, where Edmund Kean roystered with his bullyboys, the "Wolves", and later "Baron" Nicholson held his scandalous "Trials". Many of the commercial establishments were small and select, others large and varied, amongst them Hungerford Market (demolished to make way for Charing Cross Station) and Exeter 'Change, which included amongst its attractions a menagerie drawing a steady stream of sightseers, until eclipsed by the opening of the Zoological Gardens in Regent's Park. It would be fair to assert that if the Strand in Victorian times fell short of Disraeli's "finest street in Europe", it certainly offered a rich cross-section of London life and leisure.

To this variety the theatrical managers made a colourful and steadily growing contribution, especially after the abolition in 1843 of the monopoly in "legitimate" drama which Drury Lane and Covent Garden had enjoyed for the better part of two hundred years. Indeed the Strand manifestly overtook the Covent Garden district in theatrical importance as the nineteenth century progressed. The old Strand Theatre itself had its origins as a 'Panorama' opened in 1803, and operated as a theatre from 1832; almost opposite it the Strand Music Hall opened briefly between 1862 and 1866, giving place to the famous and fascinating Gaiety Theatre, with its sparkling burlesques and later on musical comedies. Edward Terry and J. L. Toole were two popular favourites who set up business in the Strand and built or christened theatres with their names. The Vaudeville, opened in 1870, still flourishes, as does the Savoy (originally fronting on the Embankment but located on the Strand and later entered from it), where the Gilbert and Sullivan operas from *Iolanthe* onwards first cast their spell over the English-speaking world. Less lasting but equally popular in its day was the nearby Tivoli, built as "the Tivoli Beer Garden and Restaurant" in 1876 and a leading London music hall between 1890 and 1914.

Undoubtedly the twin pillars of the Strand's theatre world were the Lyceum and the Adelphi. Strategically placed at opposite ends of the street, the Lyceum could be approached from either Covent Garden or Waterloo Bridge, while the Adelphi welcomed those pleasure-seekers who came by way of Westminster and Charing Cross. Both houses could boast a varied history. The Lyceum had in fact served as a venue for entertainment since 1772, but was first opened as a theatre in 1794, while a playhouse bravely calling itself the Sans Pareil was built on the Adelphi site in 1806. Both took some time to find an identity: the Lyceum, for example, provided Madame Tussaud with her first London home when she fled from Paris during the revolution, and the familiar portico was not added until the rebuilding of 1834. For the next thirty-five years the theatre enjoyed mixed fortunes, its stage sometimes graced by the appearance of such as Madame Vestris, Charles James Mathews, and the briefly brilliant Fechter, more often struggling to establish a programme and a public suitable to its standing. Both were achieved with the accession to the company of Henry Irving in 1871, for the next thirty years its luminary and for most of them its lessee. Though consistently attacked by critics and rivals, Irving's preeminence could not be denied; in the 1880s and 1890s he raised the status of the Lyceum to that of an unsubsidised National Theatre.

The Adelphi sought a less exalted role. By 1819 it had dropped

3

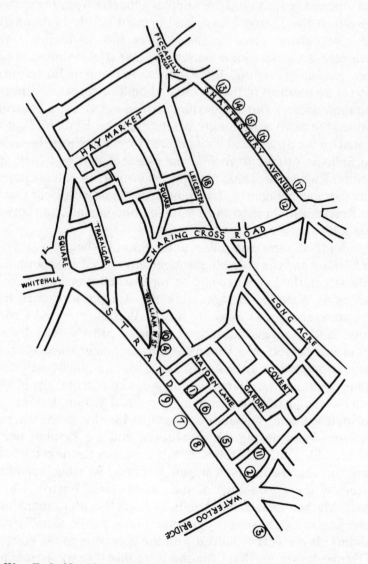

The West End of London *c.* 1890.
Key to theatres marked: *The Strand* Adelphi 1, Vaudeville 6, [Old] Gaiety 5, Lyceum 2, Tivoli 9, Savoy 7, Terry's 8 [Old] Strand 3; *William IV Street* Toole's 4, Adelaide Gallery 10; *Catherine Street* Drury Lane 11; *Shaftesbury Avenue* [Old] Shaftesbury 12, Lyric 13, Apollo 14, Globe 15, Queen's 16, Palace 17; *Leicester Square* Empire 18.

4

the name Sans Pareil, doubtless in a bid to share the prestige of the Adam Brothers' elegant Adelphi terraces, which had adorned the south side of the Strand since 1774. That bid proved only partially successful. The Adelphi had its triumphs, achieving the first recorded run of a hundred performances with a dramatisation of Pierce Egan's *Tom and Jerry* in 1821–2. But it also faced its share of crises, and underwent complete rebuilding in 1858. Many of its successes were registered under the management of the formidable Madame Celeste and her partner (when they were not quarrelling) Benjamin Webster from the Haymarket. Above all the Adelphi established itself firmly in the public mind as the home of melodrama, in the early years regularly drawn from the latest Dickens novel, hastily dramatised without the author's leave, and later often dependent on the talent as author and actor of Dion Boucicault. It was to see Boucicault in *The Colleen Bawn* that Queen Victoria paid her last visit to a public theatre in 1862, arriving and departing by that private entrance specially constructed for her in Maiden Lane which will figure prominently and fatally later in this account.

"Adelphi melodrama" in fact became a theatrical term recognised by the Victorian playgoer as promising an entertainment more stirring than subtle, more scenic than cerebral, but proudly patriotic, vigorously acted, and above all guaranteeing its public a heart-warming conclusion, with the hero vindicated, the heroine in his arms, and the villain satisfyingly seen off. Miss Prism's three-volume novel in which "the good ended happily and the bad unhappily" was evidently constructed on the purest principles of Adelphi melodrama.

That the Adelphi's means were sometimes less ample than its intentions is apparent from another common term in Victorian theatrical jargon. An "Adelphi guest" was widely employed to identify the humble "super" whose clothes and conduct fell regrettably short of the exalted character he was supposed to represent. After the withdrawal from management of first Madame Celeste and then Webster the Adelphi struggled to maintain its popularity until in 1879 the name of Gatti first appeared on the playbills as the theatre's licensees. This Swiss-Italian family became prominent amongst the entrepreneurs of the Strand in the middle of the century. Starting with a restaurant in Hungerford Market, they branched out to the increasingly popular music hall, with establishments in Villiers Street and Westminster Bridge Road. More significantly they turned the Adelaide Gallery in King William Street into the hugely successful Gattis' Restaurant. From catering to playgoers' appetites, it was a short step to catering to their entertainment, and the Adelphi was only a few yards along the Strand from the Adelaide Gallery.

The last twenty years of the century therefore witnessed the apogee of the Adelphi as a mecca for melodrama and its devotees. Success attended most of its offerings, and "Adelphi melodrama" became a cherished if sometimes ridiculed feature of theatrical London. To this success many hands contributed: the Gatti brothers, with their flair for pleasing the public; a clutch of writers (notably George R. Sims, Henry Pettitt, and Robert Buchanan, often working in collaboration) who knew that public and neither patronised their taste nor overtaxed their intelligence; scenic artists and machinists, including Walter Hann, Bruce Smith, and Joseph Harker, who rose to the opportunities their authors bestowed on them, and took shipwrecks, battles by land and sea, Derby Day or a Royal Reception, in their stride. Above all the Adelphi offered its audience a seasoned, semi-permanent company on whose abilities they could safely rely. To the knowledgeable the names of Charles Warner, Mary Rorke, Charles Cartwright, J. D. Beveridge, Harry Nicholls, and Clara Jecks guaranteed a standard of performance matching the noble principles of the play and satisfying the playgoer's demand for heroism, romance and humanity triumphing over low cunning and the vilest villainy.

For two substantial stretches during these years (from 1885 to 1889 and again from 1894 to 1897) the centre of interest at the Adelphi and the essence of its particular style and appeal was an actor whose nickname, "Breezy Bill", summed up the qualities for which his audience loved him. His real name was William Charles James Lewin, but the playbills proclaimed him William Terriss.

II: The Hero

1: Around the World

At the inquest on William Terriss the life-long friend by whose side he was stabbed while entering the Adelphi Theatre exclaimed: "I would have given twenty lives to have saved him".[1] It was no hyperbole, but a sentiment shared by everyone who knew him, on and off the stage. A successful actor, particularly a romantic leading man, is always the object of adoration – it is his capacity for being loved that in great measure makes him a leading man. But inevitably he is also the object of envy, more often than not of criticism and even hostility. Uniquely in the annals of the British stage, this was not true of Bill Terriss. When at the inquest his son declared: "He had not an enemy in the world",[2] a commonplace exaggeration was accurately used. Terriss was admired not only by the public but by the entire theatrical profession – except for an unhappy madman who, with more reason than most to be grateful to him, believed himself persecuted by the actor, and killed him.

Terriss was universally known as "Breezy Bill", and though some of his intimates – amongst them Gordon Craig – resented the nickname, it explained his universal popularity. His accepted image was Jolly Jack Tar, the hero of nautical melodrama, and it was the sailor in him, simple, sturdy, loving and loyal, that went straight to everyone's heart. Before he took to the stage he had indeed some experience of the sea and a varied career as a man of action: tea-planter, sheep-farmer, horse-breeder.

7

Unlike most Victorian actors, he neither came from a theatrical family (the Kembles, the Keans, the Terrys) nor fought his way from humble origins to great achievements (Samuel Phelps, Henry Irving). William Terriss chose his stage-name apparently at random from a street-directory. He was born William Charles James Lewin on 20 February 1847 in the well-to-do London district of St. John's Wood. His family was affluent and well-connected. His father (who died when William was only ten) was a barrister; there were lawyers, administrators and soldiers of eminence in the family, and a prestigious link through Aunt Harriet with George Grote, the historian of Ancient Greece. William's two brothers added further distinction to the family name, the elder, Thomas Herbert Lewin, serving in the Indian Army during the Mutiny, of which his published letters give a vivid account, and the younger, Friend (their mother's maiden name), pursuing a steadily successful medical career.

William was the youngest of the boys, and from early days a wanderer. By the age of sixteen he had left four schools, and was already proving something of a problem to his family. Some insight into this broken schooling emerges from a letter he wrote about 1859 to his brother:

> Windermere College
> Westmoreland
>
> My dear Friend:
>
> We have begun cricket, and I am in the fifth eleven. I have a good lot of marbles, and I have a nice little flask. I don't think I told you that I had a fight with Farie, a new fellow, about as big as Rushton, and Jip Gibson was my second; and I think I fought very well, considering you were not there. Jump and Morty backed me, and I nearly got my head broken. I wish you had been there. I am getting on pretty well, and how are you? Is your tutor a good one?
>
> Love to all,
>   And believe me,
>   My dear brother,
>   Your affectionate Brother,
>   WILLIE
>
> Write soon.[3]

No doubt it was the wandering strain in young William that suggested to his family the notion of entering him for the Merchant Navy. When he was sixteen the firm of Green and Co. took him on, providing a uniform (to the delight of the wearer) and berth (to the relief of his family). A fond farewell from Gravesend sent them tearfully but thankfully home to 6 Talbot Road, Bayswater. Two weeks later Willie reappeared on the doorstep, having jumped ship at Plymouth.[4] Painted ships on painted oceans were to prove his *metier*; the real thing was too tame by half.

These two weeks were in fact the sum of Terriss's naval service, although once his theatrical career got under way, the legend of his sea-faring days stretched prodigiously. But if he jumped ship, he retained his uniform, and wore it with what must surely have been an actor's air. For upon this uniform and this jaunty manner hangs the first well-documented episode in William Terriss's career. In the spring of 1865 his godfather, John Henry Graves (by whose side he was to be struck down thirty-two years later), invited the young man to accompany him on a Mediterranean voyage. They were to join the yacht at Weston-super-Mare, and travelled from Paddington by the night-mail in a private carriage. Their arrival in the middle of the night convinced the (surely somewhat gullible) station staff that the party was Royal, and the "cadet" in uniform no less a personage than Prince Alfred, Queen Victoria's second son, and serving in the Navy at that time. From the station the rumours spread until they overwhelmed Weston. Tradesmen left their wares at the Royal Bath Hotel where the "Prince and suite" were staying; a livery stable supplied their transport needs; the crowds flocked; the bells rocked. The episode is soberly reported in the *Bristol Times and Mirror*,[5] and clearly has a basis of truth. What gave it verisimilitude was surely the convincing performance of a leading actor in the making, playing the role of Prince Alfred.

An equally improbable but well attested episode about this time was Terriss's inheriting a legacy from an uncle "by Kentish law" (mysterious expression) at the age of seventeen.[6] This windfall he devoted in a traditionally theatrical manner to cutting an impressive figure in London. One of his means to this end was the acquisition of his own carriage (characteristically he designed it himself, and no less characteristically a friend described it as "a kind of glorified milk-cart"[7]). Before long the legacy was spent and at this point the Lewins decided – like so many Victorian families – that the best chance for the youngest son was the colonies. Since Thomas Lewin, who had soldiered in India, was by this time Deputy Commissioner of Chittagong, his young brother was despatched to Assam and put to tea-planting. Predictably he soon tired of this occupation and started for home; equally predictably his journey did not lack excitement. An account in the *Theatre* for December 1882 tells the story with appropriate flourish (and absolutely no corroboration):

> He only remained there a few months, and was shipwrecked at the mouth of the River Hooghly on his way to Calcutta. After living for ten days under canvas and a burning sun, Mr. Terriss and the few remaining survivors of the crew were picked up by a passing vessel and taken to England.

In a later interview in the *Theatre* (May 1893) Terriss dated his expedition to Assam as 1866, but made no reference to trials by sea and land.

Family counsel now decreed that William must train for a profession. An opening was obtained for him in a firm of engineers in Oxford Street, and an eye-witness recalled meeting him there "in the garb of an engine-driver, with face and hands black, and clothes which had once been white, bedaubed with grease and tar".[8] It seems pertinent to ask how an engine-driver came to be employed in Oxford Street, but whatever the reason, he was not employed there for long. At this time his brother Friend was working as a house-man at St. Mary's, and William attached himself to the Hospital's Rugby Football club, who were happy to field him at half-back, and to the Dramatic Society, who in April 1867 cast him as Fra Diavolo in H. J. Byron's burlesque, given at the Gallery of Illustration in Regent Street, later to be the cradle of both Gilbert's and Sullivan's careers.[9] Terriss's talent for friendship was immediately recognised at St. Mary's, and his close association with his brother's colleagues fostered the belief, repeated in subsequent works of reference, that he was medically trained and attended Jesus College, Oxford.

What St. Mary's could take credit for was pointing him towards a stage career. The next step in his professional education was an engagement at the Prince of Wales's, Birmingham, during the season 1867–8. His debut was marked by the physical prowess ultimately to win him fame. He "doubled" for the leading man in a tricky escape scene from Boucicault's spectacular melodrama, *Arrah-na-Pogue*. Typically he was unpaid; equally typically he lost a diamond ring in the process, and when a stage-hand found and returned it ("Bill's luck", as the actor was to say so often afterwards), he treated the finder to a brand new suit.[10]

This debut led to a speaking role, Chowser, in another Boucicault thriller, *The Flying Scud*. Overparted in this assignment, he began an important speech with "Lady Woodbee has come to Town", lost his way, could not take the prompt, but endeared himself to everyone by covering his lapse with the words "And the rest". Taking heart from Birmingham's friendly response, he decided to try his luck on the London stage. Opposite the old family home in St. John's Wood lived Squire and Marie Bancroft, the leading lights of the new drama as a result of their success in Robertson's comedies, which they were presenting at the little Prince of Wales's, off the Tottenham Court Road. Bancroft's account of his interview with the aspirant speaks for itself:

During the previous summer we were constantly told by a maidservant that "a young gentleman had called" who seemed very persistent about seeing us. One day, returning from a walk, the girl informed me that "the young gentleman" had pushed past her and walked into our little drawing-room, where he then was. I joined our visitor rather angrily, but was soon disarmed by the frank manner of a very young man, who, within five minutes, in the course of conversation, pointed to the window of a house opposite and said, "That's the room I was born in" ... Of course "the young gentleman" was stage-struck, and "wanted to go on the stage", adding that "he was resolved we should give him an engagement". His courage, and if I may say it, his cool perseverance, amused and amazed me; the very force of his determined manner conquered me, and the upshot of our interview was that I did engage him. His name was William Terriss, and Lord Cloudwrays, in *Society*, was the part in which he made his first appearance on a London stage.[12]

Lord Cloudwrays, a tiny part in the first Robertson play the Bancrofts presented, might be described in Victorian stage parlance as a "walking gentleman". After all, Terriss was a gentleman, and he could evidently walk with an air.

Perhaps the most significant comment that Bancroft makes is his admission that Terriss, although a "very young man . . . amazed and amused me . . . by his courage and cool perseverance". To have impressed London's leading actor-manager on next to no professional experience was an achievement, and points to a quality Terriss possessed from his youth: confidence. Ellen Terry, who was to be close to him professionally and personally for many years, brings this quality to life, as she does so much else about him:

> His bluff was colossal. Once when he was a little boy and wanted money, he said to his mother: "Give me £5 or I'll jump out of the window". And she at once believed that he meant it, and cried out: "Come back, come back! and I'll give you anything."
> He showed the same sort of "attack" with audiences. He made them believe in him the moment he stepped on to the stage.[13]

This story tallies with a family legend that in order to get his way he crawled out on the roof and announced he would throw himself over unless his wish were granted.

Valuable as this streak proved to Terriss the actor, it was more than "bluff", for it sprang from courage based on physical strength and freedom from fear. Terriss was an all-round athlete, but excelled particularly as rider and swimmer. Ellen Terry declares: "He was a perfect rider and loved to do cowboy 'stunts' in Richmond Park while riding to the Star and Garter".[14] His strength as a swimmer enabled him to carry out several rescues from the Thames while living at Barnes. Later he was in a rowing-boat with his son Tom while on holiday at Deal when he saw three youths in difficulties and dived to their rescue. For this he received the medal of the Royal Humane Society.[15] But the most celebrated of his rescues happened in 1893 when he was playing in *Becket* at the Lyceum, as Ellen Terry relates:

> One night he came into the theatre soaked from head to foot.
> "Is it raining, Terriss?" said someone who noticed that he was wet.

"Looks like it, doesn't it?" said Terriss carelessly.
Later it came out that he had jumped off a steamboat into the Thames and saved a little girl's life.[16]

In 1883 when the Lyceum company crossed the Atlantic on the "City of Rome" for their first American tour, a self-important passenger in yachting clothes threw his cap on the deck and offered £10 to anyone who could climb to the top of the mast with it. Terriss at once took off his coat, exclaiming: "Done! Up with you and put it on; I will follow and take it off." Had his bluff been called, he would undoubtedly have met the challenge, at whatever cost. Another glimpse of Able Seaman Terriss on this voyage is provided by Beatrice Forbes-Robertson. Mrs. Lewin, it seems, accompanied her son on the run from Liverpool to Queenstown, where she disembarked.

> As the tug cast off from the ship Terriss ran up the ratlines to the first cross-tree, hung by one hand, waved his cap in the other, and shouted:
> "Now then, boys, three cheers for My Mother!"
> The whole boatdeck burst into loud Hurrahs.[18]

And indeed William, the Sailor-Hero of *Black-Ey'd Susan*, could not have done more.

Along with this gift of bravado went an incorrigible joy in joking. The victim of his early pranks was usually his suffering but steadfast brother, Friend (known in the family as "Bob"). It was poor Bob who would repeatedly be called on to recognise a stranger in the street as "our grandmother" or "an old acquaintance, Snodgrass". Once when the brothers were travelling in an omnibus Bob, who happened to be very shabbily dressed, sought anonymity by feigning sleep, only to be roused by an insistent "My lord" for all the bus to hear.[19] Travelling with Terriss had its hazards. On another occasion he and brother Bob were travelling by train from Woolwich to Charing Cross in a compartment crowded with workmen. To this audience Terriss elected to give his well-rehearsed impression of an epileptic fit. Bob's assumption of indifference was soon questioned by his fellow-travellers, as he reports.

"I say, your mate's took bad, I think."
"Oh, it's nothing", I replied; "it will soon pass off. Leave him alone."

This response only provoked Terriss to greater efforts with a gratifying audience reaction.

"Here, I say, you must do something; he's dying."
On this cue the patient began to display such alarming symptoms that the other passengers forced his wretched companion to get out at Cannon Street in order to rush him to the nearest hospital.[20]

These stories all date from Terriss's adolescence and suggest a stage of development when acting was all one huge joke. The much put-upon Bob attended the first night of the revival of *Society* at the Prince of Wales's in September 1868, and afterwards dampened his brother's spirits by the comment: "Chuck it up, dear boy; you'll never do."[21] This was an opinion the Bancrofts appear to have shared, for when the revival gave place in January 1869 to Robertson's latest piece *School*, the "walking gentleman" was not reengaged and his brief acting career seemed to be over. The only offer made him appears to have been at Astley's Amphitheatre in Lambeth, in every sense a long way from London's most fashionable theatre. Here he represented a brigand in one of Astley's equestrian dramas, a role in which his riding skills were doubtless useful. His bluff also proved handy. The horse he rode, Teddy by name, was trained to recognise the cue: "Get thee to the mountains", and trot off dutifully. During the run Teddy died and a replacement was sought from the stables of an Omnibus Company. At his first appearance the new Teddy failed to respond to the line, and neither carrots nor cajolery could coax him into the wings. Whereupon Terriss was inspired to imitate the bus conductor's signal – three stamps of the foot and the cry: "Right behind" – and the horse moved off as required.[22]

If his riding helped him at Astley's, it was his swimming that earned him a more lasting engagement at this time. During the summer he took a trip to Margate, always a favourite spot of his, and demonstrated his skill in the sea. Amongst the crowd admiring this performance was a young lady by name Isabel Lewis, who showed commendable initiative in achieving an introduction

there and then. The immediate outcome was a stroll on the promenade. Time pressed, for the young lady was due to catch the
three o'clock train back. Such obstacles were designed for Terriss
to overcome; unperceived, he set back his watch by a few hours
and assured Miss Lewis there was time for lunch and a drive.
When they returned to the station the unbluffable clock stood
at 5.30, but Terriss brought his actor's powers to work and convinced her his watch had stopped.[23]

As their daughter, Ellaline, candidly admits, her mother "had
been on the stage for ten minutes, as it were",[24] acting under
the name Amy Fellowes. Her only documented appearance was
in the opening bill at the new Vaudeville Theatre in April 1870
when "Miss Amy Fellowes gracefully represented a Spanish gran-
dee" (according to the *Era*) in a burlesque. *Don Carlos*; *or the
Infante in Arms*. This may well not have been her first appearance
on the London stage, but it was almost certainly her last. For
in September 1870 William Terriss and Isabel Lewis were wed.
In the words of his biographer:

> The marriage took place at Holy Trinity Church, by Portland Road
> Station, and was a very quiet and unconventional function. Terriss
> had merely told his brother and his old friend, Mr. Graves, that he
> was going to be married at such a church, on such a date, and at
> such a time, and the various parties interested arrived for the most
> part by 'bus, and in everyday costume. The ceremony was performed,
> and the happy pair set out for their honeymoon at Richmond on a
> 'bus.[25]

This account suggests that the marriage was as little premeditated
as that of Mr. Wemmick in *Great Expectations*:

> Halloa! Here's a church . . . Let's go in!
> Here's Miss Skiffins! Let's have a wedding!

In fact, although Terriss's skill as a swimmer may have brought
about their introduction, the theatre probably fostered their
acquaintance. What is certain is that at the time of their marriage,
she was just twenty-one and he a couple of years older; also that
representatives of their two families were conspicuously few.

However much frowned upon, the marriage was consistently
and completely happy. Such knowledge as survives of Isabel comes

entirely from her daughter, who sketches her firmly if in the barest outline:

"She was the most unselfish woman I ever knew."

"My father adored my mother, and he thought her the loveliest woman in the world. He used to tell me when I was a child that I could never hope to be as pretty as my mother. They were such opposites – he so headstrong, she so peaceful and serene – but they matched perfectly in the marriage pattern."

"She was the only person to whom my father ever deferred."

It seems clear that their marriage, and the unfavourable view some of his family took of it, decided Terriss to abandon his desultory stage career and seek a wider field. He chose sheepfarming, not, as might have been expected, in Australia or New Zealand, but in the Falkland Isles, remote and isolated in the Southern Atlantic, and until thirty years earlier not permanently inhabited. He had, however, obtained an introduction to two brothers, by name Packe, who were starting sheepfarming in the still undeveloped East Falkland, and such a chance was an irresistible challenge to the explorer in Terriss. His wife may have seen the enterprise differently.

To reach the Falklands a six-week passage to a South American port was first necessary. This they accomplished in a Brazilian boat, the "Douro", but their point of disembarkation, Montevideo, proved to be in the throes of a revolution, and they spent ten days, besieged in their hotel. This turned out to be only the prelude to their ordeal, for the coaster "Foam", in which they then took passage for the Falklands ran into the worst of the dreaded storms for which the Southern Atlantic is notorious. Terriss's own account of this experience is given in a letter to his favourite sister, Harriet:

> Stanley
> Falkland Islands
> Monday Nov 28th 1870

My dear old pet,

Arrived well and safely at last after 18 days' sail from Monte Video in the little tiny schooner and having had the hardest and most severe passage I ever experienced, in fact had I dreamt that I should have had to put up with one quarter of what I have done I should never have left Monte Video. Well now, to give you a history of my travels – We spent a tolerably good time of it on board the Douro – and to begin with on arriving at Monte Video we found the place besieged and a bombardment going on so everything was at War prices. I had to pay a sovereign to the boatman for landing me and then the Hotel bill; luckily we had only to wait 9 days (in perpetual fear) for the schooner "Foam", and it cost me £13, so you can guess I did not take long in getting on board when the boat arrived.

Well, there was Yellow Fever raging there too. However, we got away on the 8th November – and we were not 12 hours out in the river 80 miles wide and full of Sand Banks when on comes a "Pampailla" – "awful blow" – and we nearly founded. At length we make the open sea and not 24 hours out than we are caught in the hardest gale that could possibly blow. We were hove to for 5 consecutive days, the sea running mountains high, washing everything clean off the decks and all of us "battened down" . . .

Well, with God's help we weathered it and then being 10 days out (7 or 8 days being the usual run) we ran short of food and the water had got into the casks and was brackish. However, on we went and just arrived with a bit of a breeze about 40 miles from the Island when a dense fog set in and a gale from the NW driving us fast on a lee shore. At midnight we let go the anchor in 40 fathoms' water – and it held or we were lost. Next morning – a clear sky and fair wind took us into Stanley Harbour . . .[27]

This account is as fascinating for what it omits as what is included. In her autobiography Ellaline Terriss supplies details, doubtless from her parents' conversation, her father was too considerate to provide:

... The vessel, waterlogged and in dangerous condition, was driven about 200 miles off her course. The pumps refused to work, and the only hope was – a very slight one – that she still answered her rudder and kept weigh upon herself. But most people gave up hope. They expected the ship to founder. My parents had an anxious consultation. What was to be done if the worst happened? should they go down into the depths together, or should he shoot her and then himself, to make it swift and merciful?

Certainly Terriss's modesty prevented his mentioning his own efforts in this extremity, to which his daughter pays tribute:

> ... Land was sighted and it was my father who saw it first. He had in that extremity at sea proved himself a leader of men. He had thrown himself into every job on board; he had encouraged the crew, giving them new heart by his unflagging energy, his dauntless manner ... But not even then were their troubles over. Another storm arose and drove them away – away – but their distress signals had been seen and everyone was rescued, gaunt and wan with privation and hard work – to say nothing of the fear of death – and at last the Falkland Islands were achieved.[28]

Neither account mentions that during this ordeal the hapless Mrs. Terriss was several months pregnant. As so often, the stamina of Victorian women staggers the imagination.

The sojourn of the Terriss family in the Falkland Isles has produced a wide selection of stories, some of them (such as Isabel being hailed as "Queen" by the natives and crowned with flowers[29]) transparently impossible – there were no "natives", all the settlers being European and the majority British. Terriss is reported as breaking in horses, building and sailing his own raft (which swiftly sank), dressing up as a Naval lieutenant and paying a ceremonial call on a visiting gunboat – in short doing everything except the sheepbreeding he originally undertook. That plan was put at risk from the start by his wife's pregnancy. She could not be expected to leave the "Station" (the settled West Falkland and it capital, Stanley), while her husband's commitment to the Packes obliged him to camp out on East Falkland. When the time arrived, Isabel was moved into Stanley's one hotel, the Ship (which still bears a plaque proclaiming: "Here was born the famous actress, Ellaline Terriss"), and there that greatly loved performer was indeed born on 13 April 1871. Two weeks later, by her account, she sailed with her parents on a whaler bound from Honolulu via Cape Horn for Europe.[30] Again it is the fortitude of Mrs. Terriss that commands admiration.

The family had spent five months in the Falklands, and it is clear that a wanderlust possessed Terriss throughout their stay. A postscript to his letter to Harriet, written immediately on arrival, reads: "I've written to Grote and mentioned the commission in the Cape Mounted Rifles", suggesting his thoughts were already turning towards South Africa. Ellaline's arrival turned them back to England and home. What is clear amongst the confusion of legends about this brief essay in exploration is Terriss's popularity with the settlers. The Governor stood as godfather to his firstborn, and when the family left: "We were actually taken along side the whaler in the Governor's yacht". More practically, the Governor supplied a live goat to provide a milk delivery en route.[31] William Terriss had yet to find a profession, but he had already found a public.

Their return was scarcely less eventful than the outward journey. The whaler was commanded by a Swede of such extreme misanthropy that the crew mutinied, and in Ellaline's words: "came to my father and elected him their captain". Clearly that shakily based reputation for seamanship had spread once more. Terriss's attempts to reconcile captain and crew earned him the usual reward of intermediaries. Once restored to authority, the Swede expressed his resentment by starving the Terriss family, who were reduced to slaughtering the Governor's goat. This time it was Isabel who acted as peacemaker – successfully. According to her daughter "the rest of the journey passed without incident, but in extreme discomfort, and when we arrived at Falmouth my poor mother was nearly dead from exhaustion and worry".[32] This account, though alarming enough, conflicts with Terriss's entry in *The Dramatic Peerage* (1892) which claims: "Off Gibraltar the ship was lost in a fearful gale, the crew took to their boats, and were exposed to the fury of the elements for two days before they were picked up, more dead than alive, by a passing steamer." Presumably Ellaline would know if she had been wrecked and rescued, even at the early age of three months.

In the summer of 1871 the Terriss family settled into the house on Barnes Common which was to be their home for the next twelve years. Terriss took up his theatrical connections and found himself an engagement at Drury Lane – no longer the temple of classical drama, as in Garrick's or Kean's time, but chiefly devoted to melodrama and pantomine. The company was led by an old favourite, Samuel Phelps, and a new star, Adelaide Neilson, and Terriss found himself cast as Robin Hood (an apt if minor role) in *Rebecca*, an adaptation of *Ivanhoe*, opening on 23 September. Scott in fact provided the bulk of the repertory, for after Christmas *Rebecca* gave place to *Amy Robsart* (taken from *Kenilworth*) with Terriss as Edmund Tressilian. The only widening of his experience occurred in benefit performances; in November he played the juvenile lead to Phelps's famed interpretation of Sir Pertinax MacSycophant in *The Man of the World*, and the following month obtained his first taste of Shakespeare when Adelaide Neilson chose *As You Like It* for her benefit, and he was cast as Silvius.

Drury Lane reverted to opera throughout the summer months and her actors had to look elsewhere for employment. Two supporting roles in reach-me-down romantic drama had evidently not converted Terriss to a stage career; wander-lust still possessed him, and an encounter with an old schoolfriend, one of the Tattersall family famous for horse-breeding, put into his head the notion of raising horses in Lexington, Kentucky, where another member of the family, Percy Tattersall, ran a horse agency and veterinary surgery. The idea seemed not only tempting but financially promising, and in the spring of 1872 "Izzie" and Ellaline (still short of her first birthday) found themselves crossing the Atlantic once more.[33] The decision seems to have been made on the spur of the moment, and it may be to this excursion that an anecdote related by Clement Scott, in his "Appreciation" prefacing the official biography, refers:

> He was the owner of a small cottage in a pleasant London suburb, and suddenly resolved to be off and away on one of his harum-scarum expeditions. His mind made up, the project was instantly carried into execution. Breakfast over one morning, he promptly packed up his traps, sick to death of the confinement of London life and its want of freedom. He left the place just as it was, closed the shutters, locked the door, and gave the key of the tenantless house to a neighbour. In due time the wanderer returned again, opened the cottage door, found the breakfast things just as he had left them, but now on the soiled tablecloth – a skeleton! A skeleton of what? Well, the skeleton of a poor hungry cat, that he had accidently locked into the empty house when he went away. The wretched creature had lapped up the last drop of milk and then laid down to die of starvation.[34]

The journey turned out less arduous than that to the Falklands, but conditions at or outside Lexington proved even more primitive. The Terriss family took up residence in a wooden shanty, with a yard for a kitchen and a tree-trunk for a kitchen-range.[35] How often must "Izzie" have longed for the cottage at Barnes on which they had turned the key so hastily!

Given his skill and taste for riding, it seems probable that horse-breeding appealed far more strongly to Terriss than teaplanting or sheepfarming. But it certainly proved no more profitable, and in a few months his funds were exhausted. On the other hand his family was about to increase, and as in the Falklands discretion pointed the way back. Money for their passages looked unobtainable until a local coachbuilder, J. C. Oliver, came forward with the price of three berths in steerage.[36] No doubt Terriss had business connections with him. Nevertheless Ellaline reports the benefactor as declaring: "Pay me back when you can, my boy. God speed and God bless you."[37] Again the Terriss flair for friendship had proved invaluable, while on the voyage home it also proved highly beneficial, for the rapid flowering of shipboard acquaintance produced an invitation to dine in the first-class saloon, from which the head of the family returned with tempting morsels for his wife and daughter.[38] The good-hearted coachbuilder was repaid immediately on their return, but Terriss was baulked in his determination to thank him personally. Years later, touring the States near enough to Lexington to make a detour, he sought out his benefactor, only to find he had died the day before.[39]

The Terriss family were back in the cottage at Barnes by the autumn of 1872 and back in England for good. On 28 September Ellaline's brother, Tom, made his appearance. A week earlier his father had made his reappearance at Drury Lane as Malcolm Graeme in yet another Scott adaptation, *The Lady of the Lake*. This is the first part of which a photograph has survived, and despite his tartan cloak and kilt, the young actor's moustache and centre-parting convey more of the horse-breeder than histrion. Nevertheless he caught the eye of London's foremost critic, and Clement Scott wrote:

It would be ungracious to pick the acting to pieces, because all the artists had such scant opportunity of exhibiting their talent. They were, from first to last, subordinate to and hard-pressed by the scene-painter, the carpenter, and the costumier. But fresh and pleasant, active and intelligent, enthusiastic and natural, stood out among all the rest the "Malcolm Graeme" of Mr. W. Terriss, a young actor who has now made a very fair start, and will, no doubt, do uncommonly well. The contrast between the natural and manly declamation of this young actor and the old-fashioned stilted style of some of his fellows was very striking, and it is really pleasant to find any one determined to speak as ordinary people speak, on the boards of a theatre, wherein strange tones and emphasis prevail.[40]

Encouraged by this prediction, Terriss moved in the spring of 1873 to the Strand Theatre, a modest establishment specialising in comedy and burlesque. Here he was able to extend his range by appearing in a string of short farces (though he seems to have drawn the line at burlesque), and to develop that vein of confident charm which was to serve him so well throughout his career. His modest but growing fame gained particularly from playing the hero, Doricourt, for a hundred nights from November to the following March in an old comedy, *The Belle's Stratagem* (in which, according to the *Morning Post*, "he showed his genuine artistic feelings by the sacrifice of his moustache"),[41] and filtered across the Strand to the Lyceum, where Henry Irving was rapidly establishing himself as London's leading actor under the guidance of the American impresario, Hezekiah Bateman. In a letter (now in the Harvard Theatre Collection) to one of his fellow-artists Terriss reveals that overtures were made from that quarter almost a decade before he finally joined the Lyceum Company:

> Royal Strand Theatre,
> Strand,
> 17/5/73
>
> My dear Miss Clive,
> . . . I have three different recommendations to offer you as to my capabilities the first that I have been playing leading juveniles at Drury Lane for the last two years – second that Miss Neilson offered me the engagement of seconding her in every piece she played in America, and thirdly Mr. Bateman much desired me to play De Mauprat in *Richelieu* in Sept. next, both of which engagements I was forced to decline. . . .

The Strand management held him to his contract, Bateman and Irving looked elsewhere for their De Mauprat, and in the autumn of 1874 Terriss returned to Drury Lane to play Sir Kenneth, the Knight of the Leopard (complete with leopard skin) in *Richard Coeur de Lion*, adapted from *The Talisman*. But if baulked of his Lyceum engagement, the flattering invitation and the successful run of *The Belle's Stratagem* (together with his growing family) had finally cured Terriss of his wanderlust. The young father had recognised his responsibilities; the young actor his true vocation. Henceforward the exploring would be done and the challenge met on the stage.

2: *Lyceum Limelight*

Over the next three years Terriss was steadily employed playing heroes in melodrama at Drury Lane (notably Captain Molyneux in the first London production of Boucicault's *The Shaughraun* in 1875) and elsewhere. But he owed his recognition as a leading actor to that quality of bluff or impudence which proved irresistible on and off the stage. In the spring of 1878 he was asked to play Squire Thornhill in *Olivia*, a dramatisation of *The Vicar of Wakefield*, which John Hare was staging at the small, elegant Court Theatre. On the face of it the casting seemed unlikely: Terriss had become identified with the gallant soldiers of spectacular drama. Thornhill is by way of being the villain of Goldsmith's story, the unscrupulous young squire who tricks the Vicar's daughter into a mock-marriage as the only way he can possess her. But Hare and his adaptor, W. G. Wills, approached their task in a spirit far removed from the echoes of Maria Marten this conjures up. Hare had learnt his craft with the Bancrofts at the Prince of Wales's, and Ellen Terry, who was to play Olivia, came straight from their company to the Court. The piece was thus endowed with all delicacy and persuasiveness the Bancrofts had brought to their productions of Robertson as well as older authors.

To this scheme Terriss's interpretation of Thornhill was invaluable. His effect on the leading lady was overwhelming, as she readily admitted:

> "As you stand there, whipping your boot, you look the picture of vain indifference" Olivia says to Squire Thornhill in the first act, and never did I say it without thinking how absolutely *to the life* Terriss had got it . . . It is as Thornhill that I like best to remember him.

and she concludes:

> He was precisely the handsome, reckless, unworthy creature that good women are fools enough to love.[42]

What constituted his special triumph as Thornhill was the impudence with which he contrived to make the Squire sympathetic, even loveable. Graham Robertson, the artist and intimate of so many Victorian artists, confirms this:

> His speech to the betrayed Olivia – "but if you *want* to go home, Livy, why don't you *go?*" – struck the exact note; it was no villain casting off his victim, but a bored child who didn't want to play any more.[43]

Olivia became the talk of the Town – in Ellen Terry's words: "Everyone was *Olivia* mad. The *Olivia* cap shared public favour with the Langtry bonnet"[44] – and it was after seeing her in the part that Irving resolved to make her his leading lady at the Lyceum. It seems natural to suppose that Ellen put in a good word there for Terriss, which bore fruit two years later in 1880 when he was engaged for *The Corsican Brothers*, and began an association with the Lyceum which was to last on and off for fifteen years.

Unquestionably there was a strong bond between them. They were exactly the same age – to a fortnight – and Terriss was the handsome extrovert who appealed to the woman in her, like two of her husbands, Charles Kelly and James Carew, as opposed to the artistic, imaginative men who stimulated her mind: her first husband, G. F. Watts; the father of her children, Edward Godwin; and Irving himself. It was Ellen Terry the woman, not Ellen Terry the actress, who wrote of Terriss:

> He had unbounded impudence, yet so much charm that no one could ever be angry with him. Sometimes he reminded me of a butcher-boy

flashing past, whistling on the high seat of his cart, or of Phaeton driving the chariot of the sun – pretty much the same thing, I imagine! When he was "dressed up" Terriss was spoilt by fine feathers; when he was in rough clothes, he looked a prince.[45]

The butcher-boy image is unexpected, but there is no doubt Terriss despised the airs and graces of polite Society, and projected on the stage a rugged appeal which marked him out from such contemporary idols as J. H. Barnes or H. B. Conway. The comparison with Phaeton in his chariot is more predictable. His boyish good looks wholly confounded time and grew more boyish as he advanced in years. Even in his mid-40s, when he played Edgar to Irving's Lear, he suggested to Graham Robertson "a pink and white pantomime fairy. He looked pretty and ridiculous – and most attractive".[46]

He immediately cast his spell over Ellen Terry's family – "Children, my own Edie included, were simply *daft* about him" – and she tells of

a little American girl, daughter of William Winter, the famous critic, when staying with me in England, announced gravely when we were out driving:
"I've gone a mash on Terriss."
There was much laughter. When it had subsided the child said gravely:
"Oh, you can laugh, but it's true. I wish I was hammered to him."[47]

As for her son, he came to look on Terriss as an elder brother, particularly during the time both were members of the Lyceum Company. Gordon Craig resented the facile label "Breezy Bill" – "He was a much deeper, nobler character than that nickname conveys" – and instead portrays him

erect, head splendidly carried, with brows rather like Bonaparte's ... proud, merry, but for all that as grave as a guardsman on duty.[48]

In particular he stresses Terriss's motto: "Carpe diem" – "Make the most of today" (sometimes varied to "Tempus fugit", perhaps the limit of his Latin vocabulary) and quotes a few tantalising sentences from his letters, which he often signed: "Carpe diem".

"What we spend we enjoy, but every bob we *save*, we lose."
"Carpe diem – enjoy the present."

"A pipe – and a rod and line, a good appetite and *one* friend, and you are a happy man."[49]

For Irving, who had only taken command of the Lyceum two years earlier, the accession to his company of Terriss was second in importance only to that of Ellen Terry. His forthright style was the perfect contrast with Irving's ironic, sometimes sinister, always mysterious quality. As Mercutio to his Romeo, Don Pedro to his Benedick, and later Henry VIII to his Wolsey and Henry II to his Becket, he supplied a simple strength which added depth and magic to Irving's spell-binding performance. It is also noticeable that during Terriss's second term of employment at the Lyceum from 1891 to 1894 Irving, now in his fifties, found it expedient to cast him in younger parts, thus saving himself and Ellen Terry from invidious comparisons. Terriss found himself moved from Don Pedro to Claudio, taking over Faust, and tackling Edgar in *King Lear*.

In return Irving allowed him unique privileges. No other member of the company could treat the Chief so casually. From his very first appearance, in *The Corsican Brothers*, Terriss rushed in where angels feared to tread. The last scene featured a duel in the snow-clad Forest of Fontainebleau between the ruthless Chateau-Renaud and Irving as Fabien dei Franchi, avenging his brother's death. At rehearsal the limelight-man, steeped in the Lyceum code of discipline, focussed on the star, leaving Chateau-Renaud to struggle in the dark. Terriss stopped the rehearsal.

"Don't you think, Guv'nor, a few rays of the moon might fall upon me? It shines equally, ye know, on the just and unjust."

The company held their breath. But Irving knew his man. "By all means let Mr. Terriss have a little moonlight", he replied, and kicking the salt which covered the stage, "and a little snow too".[50]

Limelight provided both literally and figuratively the aura of success in the Victorian theatre, and Terriss knew it. Making his first appearance as Nemours, the young courtier in *Louis XI* who has earned the King's enmity, he had one crucial scene with Irving in which he discovered Louis praying, Claudius-like, before plotting Nemours' death:

As the scene was arranged Irving was kneeling by the fire, with lime-light from the fire on to his face to show up his agonized pleadings, when he discovers Nemours; Nemours standing like the Angel Gabriel, but in the dark. Just before he went on, Terriss went to the limelight-man and said: "The Guv'nor says you are to put the lime on me." The limelight-man gasped. "The Guv'nor says you are to put the limelight on me", repeated Terriss. Terriss played the scene in shining armour, while Irving acted furiously in the gloom. When the curtain came down Irving exploded, but his anger melted before Terriss's ingenuous explanation: "Well, you see, Guv'nor, it was the only chance I had."[51]

The authority which surrounded the Chief never daunted Terriss. Ellen Terry relates the occasion when, goaded by his lateness for rehearsal, Irving actually reproached his subordinate:

"I think you'll be sorry you've spoken to me like this, Guv'nor", said Terriss, casting down his eyes.
"Now no hanky-panky tricks, Terriss."
"Tricks, Guv'nor! I think you'll regret having said that when you hear my poor mother passed away early this morning."
And Terriss wept.
Henry promptly gave him the day off. A few weeks later, when Terriss and I were looking through the curtain at the audience, just before the play began, he said to me gaily:
"See that dear old woman in the fourth row of the stalls? That's my mother."
The wretch had quite forgotten he had killed her![52]

She also quotes a letter he dared to write:

My dear Guv.,
   I hope you are enjoying yourself, and in the best of health. I very much want to play 'Othello' with you next year (don't laugh). Shall I study it up, and will you do it with me on tour if possible? Say *yes*, and lighten the drooping heart of yours sincerely,
                    WILL TERRISS[53]

He never played Othello for Irving, though one of his first parts at the Lyceum was Cassio in the production in 1881 in which Irving and Edwin Booth alternated Othello and Iago.
   It may be deduced that Terriss found Shakespeare a hard study.

The best known example of this concerns the passage (by no means self-explanatory) in *Much Ado About Nothing*:

> What needs the bridge much broader than the flood?
> The fairest grant is the necessity.
> Look, what will serve is fit: 'tis once thou lov'st,
> And I will fit thee with the remedy.

In rehearsal Terriss experimented with every possible emphasis.

> "What! *Needs* the bridge much broader than the flood?"
> "What needs the *bridge* much broader than the flood?"
> "What needs the bridge *much* broader than the flood?"

until Irving enquired:

> "Terriss, what's the meaning of that?"

to which the actor, according to Ellen Terry, replied:

> "Oh get along, Guv'nor, *you* know."[54]

or according to Graham Robertson:

> "Oh go along, Guv'nor; it's poetry, isn't it!"[55]

No doubt he found himself even more at a loss as Edgar in the "Poor Tom" scenes. When Graham Robertson visited him backstage, he confided:

> "It's a damned dull play you know. Damned dull. Heavy as anything", adding: "It doesn't do to take all this stuff so slow ... If you've got to say it, get it over" and "I do my best to lighten it up a bit."[56]

Yet Terriss had played Shakespeare's lovers from the start of his career. He was chosen by three leading ladies to be their Romeo: by Ellen Wallis at Drury Lane (1874); by Adelaide Neilson at the Haymarket (1879); and by the stunningly beautiful American, Mary Anderson in 1884. When Irving at the age of 44 cast himself as Romeo, with Terriss, nine years younger, as Mercutio, there was much barbed comment. Ellen Terry was asked by "a well known politician":

> "I say, E. T., why is Irving playing Romeo?"

and when she parried with "Who would you have play Romeo?" was answered:

"Well, it's so obvious. You've got Terriss in the cast . . . I don't doubt Irving's intellectuality, you know. But as Romeo he reminds me of a pig who has been taught to play the fiddle. He does it cleverly, but he would be better employed in squealing. He cannot shine in the part like the fiddler. Terriss in this case is the fiddler."[57]

Two years later Terriss did play Romeo at the Lyceum, which Mary Anderson had taken in Irving's absence on his second American tour. Like Squire Thornhill in *Olivia*, the part proved a turning-point in his career. There was no more "intellectuality" than in his other Shakespearean roles. The best that Ellen Terry could say of the performance was:

He attacked the part with a good deal of fire. He was young, truly, and stamped his foot a great deal, was vehement and passionate. But it was so obvious that there was no intelligence behind his reading. He did not know what the part was about, and all the finer shades of meaning in it he missed. Yet the majority, with my political friend, would always prefer a Terriss as Romeo to a Henry Irving.[58]

For once her evidence is suspect, since she was in North America throughout the run of the Terriss-Anderson *Romeo*. Probably she confused it with his performance opposite Adelaide Neilson in 1879. The press mostly endorsed her view:

Remembering the last revival of *Romeo and Juliet* upon these boards, one could but wish that some method of thought transference might be invented by which Mr. Irving's brains could be spirited for the nonce into Mr. Terriss's handsome head . . .[59]

wrote the critic of the *Pall Mall Gazette*, adding: "The audience, however, admired the body and did not seem to miss the brains." For the first time Terriss found himself a popular idol, recognised by a picture postcard which sold in its thousands.

At the same time his increasing success led to a move for the Terriss family (which now included a second son, William). The cottage at Barnes had grown altogether too cramped, and the Terriss clan moved to the new and decidedly artistic milieu of Bedford Park, Chiswick, a community consciously "Bohemian", yet aloof from the rivalries and jealousy of Chelsea and blessed by the District Railway with Turnham Green station, and greater accessibility than Highgate or Hampstead. Amongst Terriss's regular travelling companions after a performance were a young couple, Sydney Brough and Lizzie Webster (both from famous theatre families). Their daughter provides an attractive glimpse of him "producing new-laid eggs from his capacious pocket to help out the larder of the newly-weds".[60] In the Avenue, Bedford Park, Terriss bought a large red-brick house in Queen Anne style, oddly named the Cottage. His only concession to the artistic milieu seems to have been the wearing of a soft-brimmed hat at a time when toppers and bowlers were *de rigueur*. His preoccupations outside the theatre were wholly untheatrical: cycling and fishing, playing quoits at the West London Bowling Club, and a quiet game of cards or chess with an old friend.

Sunday afternoons were reserved for a family drive to Richmond Park in an open landau, a ritual much resented by the children.[61] But if Terriss had put aside his wandering habits, he was determined that his family should be brought up to look after themselves. Tom, the elder son, remembered their being drilled to the refrain:

> Eyes right, shoulders back,
> Heads well up in the air.
> Never look upon the ground
> But always look up *there!*[62]

Above all their father was resolved his children should be strong swimmers. There were lengthy practices at home, culminating in a journey to Margate, a boat-trip to the open sea, and the time-honoured ritual of throwing them in, one by one. It was hard lesson, but Tom at least was to be grateful for it when, at the age of sixteen, working his passage back from the States as a deck-hand, he fell overboard in mid-Atlantic.[63]

The removal of the Terriss family from Barnes to Bedford Park coincided with the actor's increasing success at the Lyceum, culminating in his tremendous popularity as Romeo opposite Mary Anderson. Irving, returning from his second American tour in 1885, sought to exploit this popularity by reviving *Olivia*, with himself as the Vicar and Terriss and Ellen Terry in their original parts. But widely as the play was welcomed, Terriss had outgrown supporting roles like Squire Thornhill. Other managements sought his services; in particular the Gatti brothers saw in him the centre-piece of their Adelphi melodramas. When the run of *Olivia* ended, he parted company – on the best of terms – with Irving and the Lyceum, and moved further along the Strand to be the star of the Adelphi. Hence forward he would be hailed as "No. 1, Adelphi Terriss".

3: *Adelphi Melodrama*

The last years of Victoria's reign marked the triumph of popular theatre in England. While audiences earlier in the century had been huge, they had also been undiscriminating and often unruly. The emergence of the music hall drew off the rowdier elements; the reputation of managements like the Bancrofts, D'Oyly Carte and Irving himself coaxed the gentry back to the stalls, which steadily absorbed what had been the pit; but the circle and galleries drew consistently on the traditional Victorian public. The era of the silent cinema was only just round the corner, ready to tempt the theatregoer by its novelty and universal availability; the demand for an intellectual drama, raised in the name of Ibsen by Archer and Shaw (and in the name of Shaw by Shaw), was beginning to fragment the audience. For the moment, however, the popular theatre remained loyal to its preferences.

Foremost amongst these was undoubtedly the melodrama. With its strong situations and stirring sentiments, it could rouse a large audience more readily than any rival entertainment. Both the Lyceum, which Terriss had just left, and the Adelphi, which he now joined, were homes of melodrama and commanded large and loyal publics. But Irving's repertoire, reflecting his highly individual style, exploited the supernatural and macabre side of melodrama. The production which followed *Olivia* at the Lyceum – a spectacular if ingenuous version of *Faust*, with Irving in his element as a glitteringly sardonic Mephistopheles – proved the biggest success of his thirty years there, running through two seasons and carrying him to further triumph in America.

Adelphi audiences looked for a more homely form of melodrama. Under the Gattis a solid, satisfying menu had been drawn up, and the patrons knew what to expect: a popular, handsome hero, disgraced or ruined by the envy and greed of a rival; separated from the girl he worshipped; exposed to extreme hardship and extraordinary danger; but ultimately exonerated and restored to his rightful position and his sweetheart's side. It was a formula which worked best against a background of the armed services, since they provided through discipline and danger the conflict such stories demanded. At the Adelphi Terriss appeared frequently as a sailor (*Harbour Lights*; *The Union Jack*; *Black-Eye'd Susan*) and soldier (*One of the Best*; *Boys Together*). He was even recruited into the U.S. Cavalry (*The Girl I Left Behind Me*); the Confederate army (*Secret Service*); and the French forces (*The Swordsman's Daughter*).

The photographs show him carrying out these various postings with conviction. Unlike some pictures of him in Shakespeare, they proclaim him entirely at ease in uniform, and in view of this Ellen Terry's comment (cited earlier) is unexpected:

> When he was "dressed up" Terriss was spoiled by fine feathers; when he was in rough clothes, he looked a prince.[64]

Perhaps her point is that his uniform did not supply the performance or the personality, and that in danger or distress, clothes soaked by sweat or sea water, the real hero of Adelphi melodrama emerged. Certainly these photographs extended his popularity far beyond the theatre itself. Following the vogue for picture postcards of his Romeo came a vogue for Christmas cards portraying him as David Kingsley in *Harbour Lights*, his first new role at the Adelphi. This vogue antedated the rage for pictures of musical comedy stars (including those of his own daughter) by a decade.

If his looks were an essential element in Adelphi melodrama, his athleticism was no less compelling. Every script exhibited his agility and prowess in some form. What seems even more striking now is the similarity between the situations devised for him and real-life episodes in his own youth. The high point (in every sense) of *Harbour Lights* (1885) was the cliff-rescue scene. David Kingsley has climbed down to rescue Lina, and both are trapped by the tide:

> (*A wave dashes over them.*)

DAVID   Ah, God, the end has come. We are lost, Lina. (*Trying to raise her*) Lina, one effort, it is for our lives.

LINA   (*slowly opening her eyes*) David, you can climb. Go and leave me.

DAVID   No, Lina, not while God spares my reason and my life to battle for us both.

(*Business worked up. The tide rises – the cliffs sink. Enter TOM and JACK in boat – as DAVID and LINA are swept off the rocks and saved!*)

The parallel with Terriss and his bride facing death in the South Atlantic is startling. In *The Bells of Haslemere* (1887) Frank Beresford strays far from Surrey and is caught in the swamps of the Mississipi:

FRANK   My brain burns. A blood-red mist is round me. What's that? The man-hunters and their hounds. No! no! they're bells. I can hear them now louder – louder still. They're tolling in the church at Haslemere. My funeral knell! . . .

(*Music begins and lights have changed to moonlight. Noise of steamer heard approaching*)

> What sound was that? It came from the river. It's the steamer coming round the bend. If they should pass me in the darkness! Help, there!

(*Calls; waves signal. A whistle from the steamer*)

> They see me! I am saved!

(*Steamer comes on at back with CAPTAIN SALEM, TOBY and REUBEN*)

PICTURE

CURTAIN

and again the young Terriss, allegedly rescued after ten days' exposure to the burning sun on the banks of the Hooghly, comes to mind.

His prowess as a swimmer was often alluded to. In *The Union Jack* (1888) Jack Medway, about to be court-martialled for striking a superior officer with very inferior designs on his sweetheart, breaks away from his escort and dives overboard:

JACK   Better death than despair like this! Hands off! I will be free!

(*Throws off MARINES. Struggle. Seized at opening again. THE ESCAPE*)

SCENE 2

(*Scene turns to Hull of Ship in Moonlight. JACK comes down by chains. Dives in the water. Boat in chase etc.*

CLOSED IN

Such exploits could be expected from the Terriss the Lyceum public had already recognised. What was unexpected in Terriss at the Adelphi was a note of simplicity and tenderness quite alien from the swagger of a Squire Thornhill or Chateau-Renaud. It was no doubt a dilution of that reckless quality Ellen Terry responded to – "the adventurous, dare-devil spirit of the roamer, the veritable gipsy" which "always looked out of his insolent eyes".[65] But, diluted or not, it won him a far wider following. In *Harbour Lights* he had to apostrophise the wedding-ring he had carried round the world to place on the finger of his devoted Dora:

Little ring, I've looked at you, and you've bidden me hope during many a long watch at sea. Now we're home again, little ring, and we are going to part. Somebody else is going to have you and keep you for ever – and you will make David Kingsley's sweetheart David Kingsley's wife.

In the autograph books of Victorian misses this passage came to assume near-Shakespearean status, yet its popularity was surely due more to Terriss than to the authors of *Harbour Lights*, George R. Sims and Henry Pettitt.

Besides the photographs of Terriss as David Kingsley there grew up romantic legends of Terriss himself. The most extravagent of these found its way into the columns of the *Theatre*. In a piece entitled "Echoes of the Pit" by "O.S.", published in August 1888, it was reported:

The first thing that occurs to me was overheard in the Adelphi during the run of *The Harbour Lights*. Seated in front of me was a lady of a certain age, who, however, had not lost her enthusiasm. She was alone but after the first act, hearing her neighbours speak of Mr. Terriss, she interposed: "Yes, is he not splendid? So good-looking, but such a sad life, my dears, such a sad life!" Her listeners at once saw that there was more behind, and eagerly asked why and how it was such a sad life. "Ah! It's a long story, but I'll just tell you the bare facts of it. Some years ago, when he was quite young, he was in Paris, gazing at the Venus di Milo, perhaps the most beautiful statue in the world. A young girl came up and also stood and gazed. Terriss turned, and then he started and looked earnestly at her, for she was the most beautiful he had ever seen. Well, it was the old, old story; he managed to get an introduction, and before a fortnight had passed they were engaged. Soon he had to go back to London to fulfil his engagement; she stayed behind to study art under one of the great French masters. Six months elapsed, and Terriss received a note from her, breaking off the engagement, but giving no sufficient reason. He hurried off to Paris, but could find no trace of her or her guardian. He never saw her again, but within a year she died, sending him a letter explaining all. She was the daughter of some great criminal, I don't know whom. She had never known this until the day she wrote, breaking off the match, saying she loved him too well to bring him dishonour. *Terriss has never married, he will never speak to a woman if he can help it, and he never acts upon the day she died."*

Of such were romantic reputations made in the days before Press Officers.

The popularity of *Harbour Lights* and its immediate successors established a well defined school of Adelphi melodrama. In the same year (1889) that Jerome K. Jerome published *Three Men in a Boat*, he also wrote a gentle spoof of theatrical conventions called *Stageland: Curious Manners and Customs of its Inhabitants*, in which both he and his artist, Bernard Partridge, drew heavily on current practice at the Adelphi. The "List of Citizens Interviewed" includes Comic Man, Lawyer, Adventuress, and Good Old Man, but is headed by a Hero who is recognisably Terriss, and which pin-points his apostrophising. In *The Silver Falls*, then running at the Adelphi, Terriss addressed not a ring but a star:

ERIC   How peaceful, how calm the evening is, even as my heart is now. Look where yonder star is, high above our heads. How many a weary night have my eyes sought that star when I have been alone, and it seemed to me to say: "Hope on, trust, be brave. There is hope, even for you, I am the star of hope."

PRIMROSE And tonight the star seems to look down on us from above and to say: "See, I did not bid you hope in vain."

Stageland censures the Hero on various counts: for his way of making love ("He always does it from behind ... he takes hold of her hands, and breathes his attachment down her back"); for his overpolished boots ("He crosses the African desert in patent leather-boots ... He takes a supply with him when he is wrecked on an uninhabited island"); but above all

> The Stage Hero never talks in a simple, straightforward way, like a mere ordinary mortal.
> "You will write to me, when you are away, Dear, won't you?" says the Heroine.
> A mere human being would reply:
> "Why, of course I shall, Ducky, every day."
> But the Stage Hero is a superior creature. He says:
> "Dost see yonder Star, Sweet?"
> She looks up and owns that she does see yonder star; and then off he starts and drivels on about that star for full five minutes, and says he will cease to write to her when that pale star has fallen from its place amidst the firmament of Heaven.[66]

Parody is often deemed proof of admiration, and ten years later Jerome K. Jerome was to demonstrate his admiration for "strong" drama by writing a ripe example, *The Passing of the Third Floor Back*.

After *The Silver Falls* Terriss left the Adelphi for five years. He first undertook a tour of North America (1889–1890) in the extraordinarily mixed repertoire that the theatrical public accepted from its favourites: it included *Othello* and *Frou-Frou*, as well as Adelphi-style melodrama. On his return he rejoined Irving at the Lyceum, where he played amongst other parts Henry VIII; Edgar in *Lear*; and Henry II in Tennyson's *Becket*. He was

Plate 1. Terriss in the Merchant Navy, *c.* 1863

Plate 2. Terriss as Malcolm Graeme, 1872

Plate 3. Terriss as Squire Thornhill

Plate 4. *Much Ado About Nothing*, Lyceum, 1882

Plate 5. Interior of Adelphi Theatre after 1858

The Stage Hero.

Plate 6. "The Stage Hero" by Bernard Partridge

Plate 7. Terriss (with Harry Nicholls) in *The Fatal Card*, 1894

Plate 8. Terriss and W. L. Abingdon in *The Fatal Card*, 1894

therefore a member of the Lyceum company which played at Windsor Castle in 1893, though the Queen, who was touchy about the stage representation of Royalty, found his King Henry "too noisy and violent".[67]

By 1894, when he returned to the Adelphi, he was 47 and perhaps felt that the boyish image of the earlier Adelphi melodramas was inappropriate. His choice now fell on more exotic backgrounds and complex roles. The American scene recurs: his first vehicle, *The Fatal Card*, opens in a Colorado mining camp with

> a view of the Rocky Mountains, through which the track of the Union Pacific Railway passes . . .

and this was followed by an American play, *The Girl I Left Behind Me* (1895), by the dictator of the American stage, David Belasco, set in Indian territory, with Terriss as Lieutenant Edgar Hawkesworth of the Tenth Company, U.S. Cavalry.

There was also a conscious attempt to give his characters greater depth. Hawkesworth, who is tormented by a secret passion, silently requited, for a fellow-officer's fiancée, is far removed from "Breezy Bill":

EDGAR   (*tears open his collar as though seeking relief in the open air*) How can I live with the heart torn from my breast? Ah! if the stars only knew I was in love with death!

Major Frank Villars in *Boys Together* (1896) discovers that his wife has in all innocence misrepresented herself as a widow. When her villainous first husband turns up, Terriss as Villars is provoked into conduct less than gentlemanly to extort the truth from him:

VILLARS   Write, or I'll pin your left hand to the table (*standing over him*).

FORSYTH   I'll not! (*trying to rise*)

            (*VILLARS, by a sudden savage movement, seizes FORSYTH's left hand and pins it to the table*)

FORSYTH   (*in agony*) Ah! (*drops as if half fainting*)

VILLARS   I'll withdraw it when you have written.

FORSYTH   You are a fiend!

VILLARS   I have only profited by your lessons. Write!

Even more tormented is Lieutenant Dudley Keppel of the Black Watch in *One of the Best* (1895), which was reviewed by Shaw as "One of the Worst", though he thought well enough of Terriss to write *The Devil's Disciple* for him. Keppel is "framed" by an enemy agent and convicted of stealing secret plans for the defences of Portsmouth. He is court-martialled, and in a scene clearly inspired by the contemporary Dreyfus case stripped of his military honours:

> *The drums begin to roll. As SERGEANT HENNESSY steps up and strips off his collar and cuffs, the drums continue to roll. As each additional mark of his rank is removed, KEPPEL's face depicts the agony which his soul is suffering.*

Unlike Dreyfus, the hero of Adelphi melodrama retained certain privileges, including the disposal of his highest honour:

KEPPEL	Stay! You may take my name, my honour, my life, but you cannot take my Victoria Cross!
SERGEANT HENNESSY	Unfold your arms!
KEPPEL	No! The cross is mine!
GENERAL COVENTRY	Quite right, the law allows it!
KEPPEL (*to MARY*)	God bless and guard you, my dear one. Ah! They would have taken my Victoria Cross, but it shall be yours. Keep it, darling, someday I shall claim it from you!

There were, however, limits to the punishment which Terriss's public could tolerate. As Vibrac in *The Swordsman's Daughter* (1895) he was presented as the father of a marriageable girl (a liberty in itself), who on discovering she is the mother of an illegitimate child, challenges her seducer. The outcome is disastrous:

> *VIBRAC and ROCHEFIÈRE get into position. They begin. Almost immediately VIBRAC takes off his mask, and lets it fall.*

VIBRAC	I can't – I won't! (*Lets his foil fall, staggers off platform and falls down, helpless and sobbing. Clamour and consternation. DOCTOR runs forward to help VIBRAC*)

MADELEINE	Father – father!
MELVIL	(*supporting VIBRAC*) Vibrac – Vibrac!
VIBRAC	(*tries to rise and speak*) My – my – daugh – (*He remains motionless, his eyes fixed on MADELEINE*)
MADELEINE	(*wildly*) Father – father! Doctor, what is it?
DOCTOR	He is paralysed.

CURTAIN

This taxed the Adelphi audience beyond endurance, and *The Swordsman's Daughter* was swiftly withdrawn. No doubt it was criticism of his more recent vehicles that decided Terriss in December 1896 to revive *Black-Ey'd Susan*, the only "traditional" melodrama he played at the Adelphi, dating back seventy years to the early days of nautical drama. He was challenging the memory of T. P. Cooke (who had fought with Nelson) as the able-bodied seaman, William, but the challenge was triumphantly overcome as he called on his messmates to "avast" and "belay", danced the hornpipe, and carried out the mysterious "back-handed wipe". During the run of *Black Ey'd Susan*, on 20 February 1897, Terriss passed his fiftieth birthday. None of his audience that night could suspect it, as he set the years at defiance. Still less did they suspect that before the year was out, he would lie, stabbed to death, on the boards he trod so lightly.

Black-Ey'd Susan herself was played by Jessie Millward, who had acted opposite Terriss in every piece he had played at the Adelphi, who was appearing with him on that fatal night, and in whose arms he died. Her part in the story of Adelphi melodrama deserves its own account.

Notes

1 *Times* 21 December 1897.
2 *ibid.*
3 Arthur J. Smythe: *The Life of William Terriss, Actor* (London, Archibald Constable, 1898) pp. 9–10 (hereafter cited as "Smythe").
4 Smythe p. 11.
5 1 March 1865.
6 *Era* 18 December 1897.

7 Smythe p. 15.
8 Smythe pp. 19–20.
9 Playbill reproduced in Smythe p. 29.
10 Smythe p. 30.
11 Smythe p. 31.
12 Squire and Marie Bancroft: *Mr. and Mrs. Bancroft: On and Off the Stage* (London, Bentley, 1889) pp. 125–6
13 *Ellen Terry's Memoirs* with notes by Edith Craig and Christopher St. John (London, Gollancz, 1933) p. 113 (hereafter cited as "Terry").
14 Terry p. 113.
15 *Era* 18 December 1897.
16 Terry p. 174.
17 Smythe p. 79.
18 Beatrice Forbes-Robertson: *Family Legend* (printed for private circulation, 1973) p. 142. I am indebted to Mr. Marius Goring for drawing my attention to this source.
19 Smythe pp. 202–3.
20 Smythe pp. 205–6.
21 Smythe p. 35.
22 Smythe pp. 63–4.
23 Smythe pp. 36–7.
24 Ellaline Terriss: *Just a Little Bit of String* (London, Hutchinson, 1955) p. 23 (hereafter cited as "Ellaline Terriss").
25 Smythe p. 37.
26 Ellaline Terriss p. 33.
27 Kindly made available to me by Mr. Robert Stuart (Terriss's great-grandson).
28 Ellaline Terriss p. 24.
29 Smythe p. 40.
30 Ellaline Terriss p. 26.
31 *ibid.* p. 27.
32 *ibid.*
33 Smythe p. 52 cites Terriss himself in dating this trip as 1871. But the source quoted refers to Ellaline as "at the time twelve months old", indicating the summer of 1872 as the correct date.
34 Smythe pp. ix–x.
35 Ellaline Terriss p. 29.
36 I am indebted to Emeritus Professor Carl B. Cone of the University of Kentucky for the information that J. C. Oliver was Master of the Lexington Masonic Lodge 1871–2.
37 Ellaline Terriss p. 29.
38 *ibid.* p. 30.
39 Smythe pp. 53–4.
40 cited in Smythe p. xii.
41 30 November 1873.

42 Terry p. 113.
43 W. Graham Robertson: *Time Was* (London, Hamish Hamilton, 1931) p. 179.
44 Terry p. 111.
45 Terry p. 112.
46 *Time Was* p. 177.
47 Terry p. 113.
48 Edward Gordon Craig: *Henry Irving* (London, Dent, 1930) p. 106.
49 *ibid.*
50 Ellaline Terriss p. 33.
51 H. A., Saintsbury and Cecil Palmer: *We Saw Him Act:* (London, Hurst and Blackett, 1939) pp. 136–7.
52 Terry p. 174.
53 *ibid.*
54 Terry pp. 173–4.
55 *Time Was* p. 176.
56 *ibid.* p. 177.
57 Terry p. 165.
58 *ibid.*
59 Undated cutting in the Garrick Club Library (Percy Fitzgerald Collection).
60 Jean Webster Brough: *Prompt Copy: The Brough Story* (London, Hutchinson, 1952) pp. 109–110.
61 Tom Terriss: TS of an unfinished autobiography, kindly made available to me by Mr. Robert Stuart, Chapter II: 14.
62 *ibid.* Chapter II: 8.
63 *ibid.* Chapter II: 11.
64 Terry p. 112.
65 *ibid.*
66 pp. 6–7.
67 George Rowell: *Queen Victoria Goes to the Theatre* (London, Paul Elek, 1978). p. 105.

III: The Heroine

The first encounter between Terriss and his future leading lady was not auspicious. It occurred at Margate (like another important meeting in his life), where Jessie Millward and her mother were on holiday in the summer of 1882. An introduction was made, and the young lady told the famous actor she was joining the Lyceum company to play Hero in *Much Ado About Nothing*. He replied: "Nonsense! You're going to walk on, and you can count yourself a very lucky girl to have even that privilege."[1]

No doubt he believed that young Miss Millward, with only a few months' stage experience, had misunderstood Irving's offer, and was concerned to spare her disappointment. But he underrated the lady, who promptly produced her "part" (Hero's lines, with cues, which was all a Victorian manager provided for his company) to prove her point. Terriss still protested disbelief, but at their next meeting, on stage at the first rehearsal, he made amends, not least by using her "family" name.

"Hullo, 'Cissie' Millward; so you *are* Hero after all." The familiarity was resented.

" 'Miss Millward' to people in the theatre please, Mr. Terriss" was her answer.

Mr. Terriss was unabashed. "Nonsense. Here's my hand; take it, and you'll have a friend for life."

As the actress wrote in her autobiography: "I took his hand, and he was my friend from that day until the terrible day when I sat holding his hand while life ebbed from the wound made by a murderer's knife."[2]

42

Unlike Terriss, Jessie Millward, who was born in 1861, came from a theatrical background. Her father, Charles Millward, was a Liverpool journalist who moved to London, where he was consistently successful as a pantomime scriptwriter. He made many theatrical friends, amongst them Irving and J. L. Toole, who were regular visitors to the Millward household. These contacts stood his family in good stead when in 1881 their father suffered a stroke from which he never fully recovered. Jessie and her brothers had to look for employment, and Mrs. Millward suggested her daughter might become a governess. But Jessie, although only twenty, had already tasted a certain measure of success in amateur theatricals, and much preferred the notion of acting for her living.

She decided to consult Mrs. Kendal, an admirable actress but a decidedly formidable lady, who offered her a walking-on part. That was not how Jessie saw herself. It was suggested that if her amateur group, the Carlton Dramatic Club, took a London theatre and persuaded the critics to review the performance, she might launch her career more auspiciously. At once she put her problem to John Toole, then starring at the Folly Theatre, off the Strand, to which he later gave his own name. Her account of the interview testifies to the warm heart and good humour of that much loved comedian.

"I want to go on the stage."

"Good!" said the old man encouragingly.

"And I want to give a special matinee."

"Splendid!"

"And – and – can I have your theatre?"

"Of course!"

The matter of a date presented difficulties. It *had* to be a Saturday, as the members of the Carlton Dramatic Club worked during the week.

"Can I have it on Saturday afternoon?"

Toole turned to his second-in-command, John Billington.

"Er – haven't *I* got a matinee on Saturday, Billington?"

"You have", said Billington grimly.

"But can't you have *your* matinee another day? You see, it's fearfully important for me."

"Of course I can" replied Toole, as if the idea was entirely

43

new to him. "Of course I can. Billington, see that things are arranged, and do what you can for her."[3]

Toole's kindness, and the efforts of Jessie and the Carlton Dramatic Club in Sheridan Knowles's comedy, *The Love Chase*, procured her several offers of work, from which she chose (in a spirit of "Told you so") one from the Kendals to play real parts with real lines. She joined their company on tour in September 1881 and made her London debut at the St. James's the following month. It was not a happy choice. Mrs. Kendal's matriarchal approach to management and Jessie's independent nature met in head-on collision. In Liverpool, for example, the audience at the Prince of Wales's, remembering her father's achievements, hailed her as one of the family. The *Era* critic wrote appreciatively:

> Miss Millward, who holds a name highly valued in literary and art circles, made her first appearance on this occasion in Liverpool as Mabel Meryon [in *Coralie*, which the Kendals offered as one of several adaptations from the French]. Her acting was distinguished by singular naturalness and marked maturity, and there need be little doubt that Miss Millward will make her place and long secure it in the theatrical world.[4]

Encouraged by the partiality of her Liverpool public, Jessie therefore made a confident entrance and kissed John Hare, the distinguished character-actor, instead of waiting for him to kiss her. Mrs Kendal sent for the sinner, dressed her down, and described her action as "the most unmaidenly performance I have ever seen in my life."[5]

Matters did not improve at the St. James's, where Mrs. Kendal was emphatically Mistress of Ceremonies. Jessie's debut as the ingenue in Clement Scott's *The Cape Mail* was noted with pride by the *Era* critic; it "justified our predictions by a clever, sympathetic and thoroughly charming portraiture."[6] But to Mrs. Kendal, who had undoubtedly risen to preeminence by a lengthy and dedicated apprenticeship, the girl was a complete beginner, indulged and flattered by a partial press. Later when Jessie joined the Lyceum company, Mrs. Kendal attended a performance of *Much Ado* and summoned Hero to her box between the acts. In two sentences she succeeded in demolishing both Irving and Miss Millward:

"I dare say you think you have done better for yourself, Miss Mill-ward", she observed consolingly. "Personally I think him laughable, and I sit in the box and smile and wonder at his success. But there is a type of girl who goes on the stage, and whose only ambition is a carriage, sealskins and diamonds."[7]

But Jessie was soon to get her own back. During the run of *Much Ado* she was driving down the Haymarket when she spotted Mr. Kendal. She stopped the carriage.

"Do tell Mrs. Kendal I have achieved my ambition. I have got a carriage at three-and-sixpence an hour. I have got a very small pair of diamond earrings, given me by my mother, and I have got a sealskin coat I bought off the wardrobe mistress at the Lyceum for eight guineas."[8]

Jessie stayed with the Kendals until May 1882, and then joined the austere but kindly Geneviève Ward who was touring in her long-proven vehicle *Forget-Me-Not*. This company she found as encouraging and instructive as the Kendals' had been inhibiting. At Sheffield, happily absorbed in her work, she returned from an outing to Chatsworth to find a letter in Irving's daunting scrawl which she was tempted to ignore. Only the interpretative skill of the leading man, W. H. Vernon, disclosed that it was an offer to play Hero in the forthcoming Lyceum production of *Much Ado About Nothing*, and only Geneviève Ward's insistence moved her to accept.

At the first rehearsal her usual confidence deserted her, but Ellen Terry promptly took her under her wing. "You'll hold my hand all through this rehearsal, and tomorrow you will be able to walk alone." Jessie had the grace to admit:

It was many a day before I learnt to "walk alone" in my art, and never should I have done so but for the wonderful kindness, patience and sympathy of those great artists and great teachers, Henry Irving and Ellen Terry.[9]

Nevertheless she was unquestionably a headstrong girl, who liked her own way. In the spring of 1883 when the company was running through the repertoire for the first American tour, she discovered that as the ingenue in *Louis XI* she was expected to wear a dress made for Virginia Bateman ten years earlier. An appeal to Loveday, the company manager, produced no satisfaction. Before long she was in Irving's dressing-room in a flood of tears.

> "*Of course* you shall have new dresses" he said soothingly, and sent for Mrs Reid, the wardrobe mistress.
> When all was settled, he asked:
> "And now, my child, are you quite comfortable?"
> "Oh *yes*, Mr. Irving, thank you very much."
> "Quite sure you're comfortable?"
> "Oh, quite sure."
> "Then that's all right, because you're sitting on my spurs."[10]

During the run of *Much Ado* and the American tour which followed, the friendship of Jessie Millward and William Terriss, inaugurated by that handshake at the first rehearsal, grew and flourished. He protected her at rehearsals when she could not produce the effect Irving required, by caricaturing the Guv'nor's walk (often compared to a crab's crawl) before his very face. When the company boarded the "City of Rome" at Liverpool, he impressed her enormously by confiding:

> "Understand, it is a rule of the sea that the women and children go first, and you shall be the first. I've got a pistol in my pocket."
> "Good heavens, are we going to be wrecked?" I blurted.
> "One never knows", he replied darkly.[11]

On board he made her his accomplice in various "bluffs", notably a hypnotic act, originally devised as a joke at the expense of a prim lady in the company, which "built" to a major demonstration before the whole of the passenger list. She was with him on the near-fatal trip to Niagara Falls when Terriss slipped and all but fell. He was quite unshaken. Encountering Ellen Terry on stage that night, he murmured: "Nearly gone, dear. But Bill's Luck. *Tempus fugit.*"[12]

Perhaps it was this quality of nonchalance that appealed to her. There were after all plenty of dashing and eligible *young* men in the Lyceum company – including at various times Frank Benson, Martin Harvey, Johnston Forbes-Robertson, and George Alexander. But it was Terriss, fourteen years older than she, who attracted her. When the company returned to London, she decided to make a break. She went to Irving and asked to be released from her contract.

> He reminded me that, although I was not actually playing at the moment, I was still a member of his company, and then sat silent for a time, looking at me.
> "Yes", he said at last, quietly, thoughtfully, "you can go; perhaps it will be better for you to go – for a while. But I want you always to look upon the Lyceum as your home – a home you can always return to."
> He knew and understood far better and far more than I myself at that time.[13]

In fact she had decided to put the Atlantic between herself and the Lyceum. Daniel Frohman, the American impresario, had spotted her on the tour and offered her a leading role in New York. At the same time Terriss decided not to accompany Irving to the States that autumn, a decision which led to his appearance opposite Mary Anderson in *Romeo and Juliet* at the Lyceum. Nevertheless he did not forget her. When the Gatti brothers offered him a starring engagement at the Adelphi a year later, the question of a leading lady arose. Jessie had not played in London for two years, and her standing with the London public was that of a newcomer. But Jessie was offered the position of leading lady at the Adelphi. She was playing on Broadway when she received a cable from Terriss. This time there was no hesitation; she went straight to Frohman, obtained her release, and cabled back: "Sailing in a week."[14]

The photographs of Jessie Millward scarcely suggest the fragile heroine of melodrama. She was in no sense an English rose. With her dark complexion, dark hair, brown eyes, a figure on the full side even in her youth, and growing fuller, she looked more Latin than Anglo-Saxon. But the contrast with Terriss – pale complexion, blue eyes, spare figure – was complete and mutually beneficial. There is no doubt that her lively temperament and spirited playing did much for the ill-used Adelphi heroine, whom authors consistently starved of dramatic interest, often to the advantage of the "adventuress" or "woman with a past" who figured prominently in their plots. The heroine's function was to wait until the

hero finally overcame all obstacles and claimed her. If she was
an heiress, she spent the intervening period in Good Works. In
Harbour Lights, Dora, the first Adelphi heroine Jessie created,
is clearly cousin to Rose Maybud of *Ruddigore*. Rose, it will be
remembered, provides "some peppermint rock for old Gaffer
Gadderby, a set of false teeth for pretty little Ruth Rowbottom,
and a pound of snuff for the poor orphan girl on the hill". Dora
seems similarly forgetful:

> ... I've been giving out my weekly allowances of tea and sugar to
> the old folks. The jelly I made for the sick – and the tracts which
> the parson gave me for the wicked – but I've made such mistakes.
> I've left Mrs. Jones, who's a teetotaller the sherry – and the tobacco
> for old Preston I've given to Mrs. Smith's baby.

Harbour Lights was running triumphantly at the Adelphi in 1886
when Gilbert wrote *Ruddigore*.

The heroine without a fortune had only her hopes to live on,
and suffered proportionately. The most persecuted of Adelphi
heroines was undoubtedly Ethel in *The Union Jack*, who is taken
to "a private nursing-home", drugged to facilitate the evil designs
of Captain Morton, escapes, and wanders halfway round Kent
in a snowstorm before finally being rescued by the intrepid Jack
Medway. It is presumably Ethel's sufferings in the snow that
prompted Jerome K. Jerome's observations in *Stageland*:

> "One thing that must irritate the Stage heroine very much on these
> occasions is the way in which the snow seems to lie in wait for her,
> and follow her about. It is a fine night before she comes on the scene;
> the moment she appears it begins to snow. It snows heavily all the
> while she remains about, and the instant she goes it clears up again,
> and keeps dry for the rest of the evening.
>
> The way the snow "goes" for that poor woman is most unfair. It
> always snows much heavier in the particular spot where she is sitting
> than it does anywhere else in the whole street. Why we have sometimes
> seen a heroine, sitting in the middle of a blinding snowstorm, while
> the other side of the road was as dry as a bone. And it never seemed
> to occur to her to cross over.
>
> We have even known a more than usually malignant snowstorm to
> follow a heroine three times round the stage, and then go off R. with
> her.[15]

But rich or poor, the Adelphi heroine faced fates worse than death in every play, comforted only by the knowledge that her hero was waiting in the wings. Thus Dora in *Harbour Lights* comes as near seduction at the hands of Squire Morland as any leading lady could be asked to do:

SQUIRE   Dora Vane, you leave this house as my affianced or you shall never hold up your head before the world again. (*Clasps her in his arms and kisses her*)

DORA   Help, help! (*She breaks away and rushes to folding doors at back, as SQUIRE intercepts her and fastens them*)

SQUIRE   Not this way, my pretty bird. (*Business worked up, she rushes to the window, draws aside the curtain and throws open the window as DAVID appears, who throws down the SQUIRE and takes her in his arms*)

DORA   David, thank God!

DAVID   Lie there, you hound! Come, Dora, this is no place for you!

On the other hand Jessie Millward's position as leading lady at the Adelphi gave her some of the privileges which queens of musical comedy were to enjoy in the next decade. There were numerous stage-door admirers with every gift the jeweller and florist could provide. She writes most touchingly, however, of a fan whose offering took the form of a racing tip, the name of the horse and a signature "From your admirer" twisted into the form of a cocked hat. Occasionally the racing tip was varied to a Stock Exchange tip. Eventually she persuaded the stage-door keeper to describe him.

"He's a very shabby and a very little, elderly man, miss. And he always says: 'There's no answer.'"

Jessie asked the stranger to leave his name so that she could thank him. A few days later she enquired if her message had been delivered.

"Yes, miss, but he wouldn't leave his name. All he said was: 'She wouldn't know me, and she wouldn't want to.'"

Jessie and William Terriss were to play opposite each other

at the Adelphi for more than a dozen years and a dozen plays. Predictably their professional partnership flowered into a close personal relationship. In her autobiography she refers to Terriss as "my comrade", and it sounds the appropriate note for their friendship. Victorian theatre families were accustomed to such situations – there was precisely the same understanding between Charles Wyndham, star of the Criterion, and his leading lady, Mary Moore, ultimately to become the second Lady Wyndham. Spared the exposure of modern gossip columnists and television cameras, the comradeship between the Adelphi's leading players did not imperil the unity of the Terriss family. Jessie was established with her faithful maid, Lottie, in a flat in Prince's Street, between Regent Street and Hanover Square, and this Terriss used as his West End base. "Izzie" and the children accepted the professional advantages of the partnership and welcomed Jessie as a friend. Ellaline in particular remained on the most affectionate terms with her, and Jessie included in her book one of the many loving messages she received from her, long after the murder:

> My dearest Jessie,
>   My thoughts will be with you on Christmas Day, and I shall say a prayer for you at Brompton tomorrow. I wish it were in my power to make you happier, but I fear it is not. However, you may always feel, *I love you*.
>
>   ELLA[17]

In addition to their Adelphi partnership, Terriss and Jessie frequently undertook Shakespearean recitals, and in 1889–90 headed a company which toured North America. On their return Terriss rejoined at the Lyceum and Jessie tried to follow an independent career, appearing in several Drury Lane melodramas, but separated from Terriss she found neither happiness nor success, and eventually in 1893, pocketing her pride, went to Irving and persuaded him to let her take over the small (and far from sympathetic) part of Queen Eleanor in *Becket*. This engagement took her on another American tour with the Lyceum company, and ultimately in the spring of 1894 to what she claimed was the most rewarding role of her career: replacing Ellen Terry as Margaret in *Faust*, with Terriss as Faust. Initially the audience's resentment at the substitution upset her, but Irving, playing Mephistopheles, had a highly effective antidote ready:

> As Margaret knelt praying in the Cathedral scene, a bony finger gave her two or three severe prods, and a well known voice muttered, *sotto voce*:
> "Louder! – louder! More agony! more agony!"

On the Saturday, with a matinee and evening performance behind them, Irving turned to her as the curtain fell:

> "Like to play it all over again?" he asked.
> "I should!" I cried.
> "I really believe you would" he chuckled.

But then, as she herself adds, the Mephistopheles was Henry Irving and the Faust William Terriss.[18]

When later that year the Adelphi reclaimed them both, Jessie's roles underwent a transmutation comparable to those of her partner. The Adelphi heroine, hitherto a stay-at-home, began to travel more widely. In *The Girl I Left Behind Me* she was Kate Kennion, an American General's daughter, unhappily engaged to one Cavalry officer while responding to the silent worship of another. The climax of Belasco's play taxed her powers to the full. The Garrison is surrounded by hostile Indians whose designs on the womenfolk are all too predictable. In the climactic scene, owing much to Boucicault's *Relief of Lucknow*, Kate faces death at her father's hands rather than disgrace at the Indians':

KATE   (*kneeling*) "In the midst of life we are in death."

           (*KENNION, with an agonised look, faces her*)

           "Of whom may we seek for succour, but of Thee!"

           (*During a moment's stillness the distant notes of the bugle call to "advance" are heard very faintly, off. Lets her uplifted hands fall across her eyes and*

KATE   Now!

           (*KENNION, with a heartbroken cry, clicks the pistol, which is held at his right side. The weapon must not be seen by the audience. The bugle is heard again, more distinctly but still distant. KATE vaguely begins to hear* it – *as KENNION is about to raise the pistol which is still unseen, she utters a cry*)

KATE   Listen – listen! Do you hear it?

KENNION What?

KATE   Sh! (*straining every nerve*) I hear the call of the Twelfth!

KENNION Impossible! (*The bugle call is heard nearer*)

KATE   There! Now do you hear it? Help at last! (*wild with joy*) They are coming! They are coming!

(*The bugle call of "Charge" is sounded close at hand*)

KENNION Thank God!

(*A low volley fired by the approaching relief party is followed by a general commotion. KATE, laughing and sobbing hysterically, seizes the flag, dashes on to the parapet, and waves it frantically. Wild cheering in barracks. EDGAR, with mud and dust on his uniform, enters L.U.E.*)

EDGAR   (*saluting*) General!

(*KATE at the sound of EDGAR's voice staggers down from the parapet, still carrying the flag. When she realises he is alone, she sinks across KENNION's breast, extending her hand towards EDGAR, who grasps it*)

CURTAIN

Edgar was the silent worshipper, and of course Belasco had arranged for him to claim Kate's hand in the last Act. Terriss was playing the part.

Jessie's other roles during this second phase of Adelphi melodrama made similar demands. In *Boys Together* she was the (innocently) bigamous wife, denying her second husband her bed and tackling a sleep-walking scene without Shakespeare's assistance. The climax seems to have impressed Conan Doyle sufficiently to be reproduced at the Reichenbach Falls. Forsyth, the villain, and Villars, the hero, battle to the death on an Alpine peak:

FORSYTH At last! You shall go to hell alone!

(*with an effort to turn him over – VILLARS by swinging round defeats him*) No! Then we'll go together! (*wildly*) We were boys together, you know – let's die together! (*with an effort to fling himself over with VILLARS*)

VILLARS   (*throwing himself back but falling on the edge with FOR-SYTH*) Fool! Madman! I had forgiven you!

FORSYTH   Too late! I hate you! Come with me! Come with me!

      (*They roll over together; FORSYTH out of sight screams; VILLARS' hand is seen clinging to a piece of projecting rock*)

But Jessie, as befitted the widened horizons of the Adelphi heroine, was on hand to save her man:

      ... ETHEL, who has rushed back from the pathway, at the commencement of the struggle, now enters and runs upstage.

ETHEL   Frank! Frank! (*She kneels at the edge of the precipice*) ... Quick – take my hand – I will help you!

VILLARS   (*faintly*) No, no! Keep away! I would only drag you over!

ETHEL   I must save you – I will – I will!

and with the aid of "a long hooked stick which is standing against the penthouse" she duly does so.

After the demands made on her in such pieces, it must have been restful to return to the old passive role of the heroine in *Black-Eye'd Susan*. The choice of Jerrold's long-standing favourite underlines the difficulty of finding new plays with parts suitable for both the Adelphi's stars. A proposal that they follow *The Girl I Left Behind Me* with another piece by Belasco, *The Heart of Maryland*, was vetoed by Terriss because the heroine was required to cling to the clapper of a bell which would announce her lover's escape. He saw no reason to expose Jessie to such danger. Even seasoned practitioners of Adelphi melodrama like George R. Sims seemed to be deserting the partnership. Learning that his latest piece had been secured by another management, Terriss cabled to him with unconscious percipience:

Sorry to hear world rights sold. How about next world's?[19]

It must have been in this emergency that Terriss conceived the idea of collaborating with the young critic of the *Saturday Review* who had demolished so many popular plays of the day but was known to write for the stage himself. Early in 1896 he sent for

Shaw and outlined a scenario in which "he is arrested for forgery or murder at every curtain, and goes on as fresh as paint and as free as air whenever it goes up again" (so Shaw later wrote to Ellen Terry). When the scourge of the profession demonstrated that there was too much sensation and not nearly enough sense, Terriss meekly answered: "Mr Shaw, you have convinced me", and threw the script into the fire. Shaw then offered to provide a suitable vehicle from scratch, and the outcome was *The Devil's Disciple*, in essence an orthodox Adelphi melodrama with tailor-made parts for Terriss as Dick Dudgeon and Jessie as Judith Anderson.[20]

The finished product was unveiled to Terriss one afternoon at Jessie's flat in Prince's Street. It was one of those occasions when destiny contrived to thwart an eminently workable project. Shaw insisted on reading his own script, not knowing that Terriss utterly abhorred such proceedings, and much preferred to judge a play by reading it for himself. Jessie, well aware that a few pages read in Shaw's lilting Irish tones would lull her colleague into slumber, desperately struggled to keep him awake by constantly interrupting the reading with suggestions that they change places, as she was cold. Her efforts were of no avail. At the end of Act Two Terriss woke up and said:

> "No, Shaw, no, I'm afraid it won't do. I don't like the end. It isn't suited to Miss Millward and myself."

Understandably incensed, Shaw replied:

> "Mr Terriss, I have not finished the play, and I am not going to finish it."

Trying to avoid a total breakdown, Jessie rang for tea. Terriss suggested a whiskey, to be answered with a frigid:

> "I never drink anything but water."

The idea of a meal was even more summarily dismissed, the offended author declaring: "I never eat meat". Finally he pocketed his script and departed on the exit line:

> "I didn't have you in mind for the part, Mr. Terriss. I wanted Miss Millward, and I hope that one day she will play in one of my pieces."[21]

In the end the Gattis, despairing of finding a suitable successor to *Black-Eye'd Susan*, offered the Adelphi to the American, William Gillette, who brought his own company in his own play, *Secret Service*, with enormous success. Terriss was therefore free to accept an invitation from Cyril Maude, actor-manager at the Haymarket, and his wife, Winifred Emery, to appear in a period comedy called *A Marriage of Convenience*, opening in June 1897. It might more accurately be described as a divorce of necessity, since there was no part in it for Jessie. The public frowned on the separation; the convenient marriage was soon dissolved, and when Gillette and his compatriots returned to New York, the Gattis decided to revive *Secret Service* with Terriss and Jessie heading an English cast. The story, set in Richmond, Virginia, the Confederate capital, during the last months of the Civil War, provided suitably strong situations. Terriss as the Northern "spy" who had infiltrated the Southern command, only to find himself forced to shoot his own brother, replaced Gillette. Jessie was welcomed back as the Southern belle who loves and protects him despite her suspicions of his identity and loyalties. Of course the press compared them unfavourably with their American predecessors, but the public made no such reservations.

By September 1897 a new vehicle, set against the background of the Napoleonic Wars, was ready for them. However, *In the Days of the Duke* suffered from the fate of most works which exploit the historical realities of the Duke of Wellington and the Battle of Waterloo. The invented characters and incidents paled into insignificance beside their real-life rivals. Terriss was required to play both father (in the Prologue) and son, the latter much addicted to drink and dissipation, although finally purged by heroism on the battlefield, but the complicated story was submerged beneath an excess of military history and display, and the run ended abruptly in November. Once more caught without an attraction, the management decided on a revival of *Secret Service* over the Christmas period.

The hectic tempo and desperate search for acceptable entertainment during the summer and autumn of 1897 left Jessie depressed and full of foreboding. She found her sleep increasingly troubled by nightmares; in particular a dream that she could hear Terriss crying out: "Sis! Sis!", and that after searching for him and tracing his cries to a locked room, she would burst open the door and catch him as he fell.[22] The dream recurred with such vividness that she told him of it, and begged for a keepsake in case of catastrophe. Terriss as always took a commonsense view of her imaginary fears, but went so far as to offer her his watch and chain, an offer she felt too self-conscious to accept. Her peace of mind was further disturbed by a number of stage-door encounters with "a short, thin, dark man with a pronounced squint whom, when he was employed as a super, I had often seen posing about the stage." One night she actually heard the unwelcome visitor's voice raised in Terriss's dressing-room, and on questioning the purpose of his visit, was told: "This man is becoming a nuisance."[23]

On the afternoon of Thursday 16 December Terriss brought his life-long friend, Henry Graves, to the Prince's Street flat. They had been playing poker with Fred Terry at the Green Room Club. Jessie provided them with a meal and left them playing chess, while she and her maid went ahead to the theatre. Her usual practice was to let herself in by the "private" entrance in Maiden Lane, but on arrival there she caught sight of the "short, dark man" loitering across the street. "There was something in the man's face that frightened me", she recalled afterwards, "and instead of waiting to open the pass-door, I rushed to the stage-door".[24] At that date this was situated in the narrow passage between Maiden Lane and the Strand. She climbed the stairs to her dressing-room which overlooked Maiden Lane and was immediately above the pass-door. With Lottie's help she began to prepare herself for the part of Lilian Varney.

"In the midst of my dressing I heard Mr. Terriss put his key in the pass-door, and then there was a strange silence."

Notes

1 Jessie Millward (in collaboration with J. B. Booth): *Myself and Others* (London, Hutchinson, 1923) p. 64 (henceforth cited as "Millward").
2 *ibid.* p. 65.

3 *ibid.* pp. 52–3.
4 28 September 1881.
5 Millward p. 55.
6 27 October 1881.
7 Millward pp. 56–7.
8 *ibid.*
9 *ibid.* pp. 64–5.
10 *ibid.* p. 69.
11 *ibid.* p. 82.
12 Terry pp. 220–1.
13 Millward p. 102.
14 *ibid.* p. 108.
15 p. 17.
16 Millward p. 123.
17 *ibid.* p. 237.
18 *ibid.* p.187.
19 George R. Sims: *My Life* (London, Eveleigh Nash, 1917), p. 271.
20 Christopher St. John (Editor): *Ellen Terry and Bernard Shaw. A Correspondence* (London, Reinhardt and Evans, 1949), p. 230.
21 Millward pp. 117–18.
22 *ibid.* p. 229
23 *ibid.* p. 230.
24 *ibid.*

IV: The Villain

At his trial the murderer of William Terriss was invariably referred to as Richard Archer Prince, actor. His victim, on the other hand, was named as William Charles James Lewin, otherwise William Terriss.[1] Yet for nearly thirty years Lewin had been known throughout the English-speaking world as Terriss, while Prince was a stage-name adopted only half-way through the actor's inglorious career. It is as though the law acknowledged the prisoner's assumption of a fantasy-identity, having cast off the humble reality of his birth and breeding.

That reality emerged as soon as Mr. Sands opened the case for the defence. Margaret Archer deposed that she was the second wife of a Scots farm-labourer and that the accused was her eldest child. She gave the year of his birth as 1858, and although at the time of the trial his age was consistently reported as 32, his mother seems likely to have known best. Soon after he was born:

> She was in the harvest field and left her baby in order to do some work. It was a very hot day. When she returned he was blue in the face and his eyes were bad. She took him to a doctor. After that sunstroke he was a little bad-tempered.[2]

It was an unhappy start to an unhappy existence. There were already strains of madness on the father's side – one half-brother, David, was born insane, and another brother, James, died in a mental asylum. But in Richard's case the madness took the form of a driving ambition to be a leading actor, an ambition which neither dissuasion nor failure could shake.

Apprenticed to a Dundee shipbuilder, the young Archer spent all his spare time and any spare cash at the local Theatre Royal. A couple of years' dedicated playgoing brought their reward in the form of a "walk-on", swelling the ranks of a visiting company. From that time forward he sought every occasion to appear either at the Theatre Royal or the newer and grander Her Majesty's. Failing these he would turn to any "penny-gaff" that would use him, although such appearances were solely for his own satisfaction. His living was still in the shipyards.

But about 1878 when he was nineteen or so, one of his half-sisters returned from London to the modest family home. This sister, whose name is only recorded as "Mrs. Archer" (a surprising coincidence if true), was to play a key-role in Richard's story. She was evidently possessed of more looks than principle. Years later he pointed to a striking beauty in an illustrated magazine and exclaimed to a colleague: "That's my sister. We are considered the handsomest family in Scotland", adding "It's only this secret sorrow that has made me what I am."[3] The illustration may not have been of the lady but her attractions were enough to keep her in some style. There is a lack of evidence that she was ever married, and "Mrs. Archer" suggests a *nom de conveniance*.

At any rate she persuaded her father and step-mother to remove from Dundee to her establishment in London, where they were joined by the stage-struck Richard, determined to pursue his theatrical career in the capital. In this aim he was eventually successful, and at the theatre with which he was to be fatally linked. His first London appearance for which any scrap of evidence exists was in *Michael Strogoff* (adapted from Jules Verne) in 1881 – at the Adelphi.[4]

Had he not, nearly twenty years later, murdered William Terriss outside that theatre, Richard Archer's stage-career would have been written in sand. Even so, the prints are faint and far apart. There is no conclusive evidence that he ever spoke a single line on the Adelphi stage, He was unquestionably a member of a pool of "supers" on whom the management drew, but such humble participants rarely figured on the playbill. Even his best documented appearance – in *Harbour Lights* – goes unrecorded in the programme. This play was probably Terriss's biggest success

at the Adelphi, and amongst other unsung "supers" was a C.
St. John Denton, later to turn agent and in that capacity to search
vainly for employment for his fellow-extra, Richard Archer. Denton recalled that when he joined the *Harbour Lights* company:

> I understood he had been there some time. Indeed we looked on
> him as a "standing dish". He dressed in the same room with me . . .
> I had ample opportunity of noting his eccentricities . . . He had a
> brogue that you could cut . . .[5]

But even at this stage Archer had conceived that disastrous jealousy of the Adelphi's leading man which was to ruin both their
lives. Denton adds:

> He possessed a great histrionic ambition, and was in fact a dressing-
> room butt . . . He used even then to express animosity against Terriss,
> and it was common chaff to say: "No doubt you ought to occupy
> his position."[6]

Harbour Lights, it may be noted, opened in December 1885,
twelve years before Archer knifed the man he so envied.

Tracking down the mute, inglorious appearances of this dressing-room butt presents countless problems. There is, for example,
the basic difficulty of his name, even when the playbill deigns
to mention it. A "Mr Archer" played O'Flanigan in a successful
Adelphi piece, *In the Ranks*, in 1883, and we have the author's,
George R. Sims, word that this was the assassin of William Terriss:

> Prince or Archer – that was the name we knew him by at the Adelphi
> . . . was known to many members of the profession as "Mad Archer"
> . . . While in a small part in *In the Ranks* he complained to me twice
> that another actor was trying "queer" him . . .[7]

"Mr. Archer" also appeared as Lanty in the revival of Boucicault's
Irish drama *Arrah-na-Pogue* which, though brief, established Terriss as the star of the Adelphi firmament. Although there is ample
testimony that Archer appeared in both *Harbour Lights* and *The
Union Jack* over the next few years, theatrical record does not
acknowledge his participation.

But when *The Silver Falls* opened in December 1888, a "Mr.
Prince" figures on the bill as "Diego". The announcement is historic, though not for theatrical reasons. Diego does not rate a

mention of any kind in the text of the play, but is presumably one of the bystanders at the wedding celebrations in Act II. "Work up to Mexican Dance" runs a stage-direction laconically. On the other hand the emergence of a Royally named (however silent) "Mr. Prince" in place of the humbler "Mr. Archer" (with "a brogue you could cut") is of some significance. Even if the Flanigans and Lantys lacked lines, their impersonator's brogue presumably added something to the flavour of the crowd scenes. But at some stage in the many gaps of Archer's record during these years he underwent a change of accent as well as name. In this connection it may be helpful to note an observation by one Harry Percival, an actor who toured with him in *The Union Jack*. Percival asserted that Prince "was employed at some time as secretary or valet, most likely the latter, to an officer in the Guards", adding that by that time (the early 1890s) he "spoke with a slight foreign accent".[8] It seems highly probable that in dropping the Scots brogue of Archer and adopting the exotic accent of Prince, the former valet was cultivating His Master's Voice.

In more ways than one *The Silver Falls* marked a turning-point in Richard Prince's history. It also marked a break with his family, for about this time his mother returned alone to Dundee, presently settling in the home of a stepgranddaughter. Probably her husband had died, and the tenuous link between mother and sophisticated stepdaughter was severed. The simple, semi-literate woman revealed in newspaper accounts ten years later can have had little in common with an attractive London lady of easy virtue. On the other hand her son had no incentive to return with her. After establishing some sort of grasp, however precarious, on a stage career, he was reluctant to leave London, although further offers, even of crowd work, did not materialise. Ironically, the departure from the Adelphi on an American tour of the envied Terriss coincided with the dropping of the obscure "super".

Failing a London engagement, there was available in the late Victorian theatre a wide variety of provincial work, and here Prince's experience at the Adelphi, however modest, served him well. In fact it was to "R. A. Prince, late Adelphi Theatre" that such offers as the actor subsequently received were made. In particular he established a connection with J. F. Elliston, a provincial manager of some repute, based in Bolton but touring companies throughout the North of England and Lowlands of Scotland. One of his most profitable productions, regularly revived, was an Adelphi favourite, *The Union Jack*. It was in this play and in the modest role of the Sergeant (for which presumably he sacrificed his foreign accent and reverted to a Scots brogue) that Prince chiefly appeared in the early '90s. There were other plays and other parts, but *The Union Jack* recurred.

Elliston appears to have been a loyal and understanding manager who kept a nucleus of actors employed from season to season. Consequently when news of Terriss's murder broke, reporters had no difficulty in tracking down Prince's colleagues during these years, and obtaining their views of the assassin. These varied from a laconic

> "We used to throw things at him and so on, just in pure friendliness, you know" and "You know the sort – 'Amlet-struck and Othello-struck"

to the fuller

> "He thought himself a great actor, simply because once or twice he got a couple of lines to speak. 'My lord, the carriage waits', and that class of work. Wanity, disappointed wanity and ambition – that's wot I calls the reason of it."[9]

Clearly Prince made an uncongenial colleague. Her Majesty's, Dundee, figured on Elliston's itinerary, and an official there, Robert Beveridge, gave evidence at the trial that "he had a quarrel with other members of the company. The prisoner cursed and swore more than other people."[10] Obviously he was trying to cut a theatrical dash in his home-town. Another colleague, Harry Percival, was kinder, asserting that Prince "was an excellent worker and capable enough in his own way, but always looked on as a bit of a madman". As evidence of this he added that the actor "claimed intimacy with the Prince-of-Wales, and spoke of himself as brother-in-law to the Emperor of Johore". Also "he would sit at the piano and sing stupid songs to the most discordant accompaniments, and give imitations of actors he had seen, Mrs Bernard Beere, for instance". Most ominously, he repeatedly stated: "If a man did me an injury, I would rip him up."[11]

Plate 9. Terriss and Jessie Millward in *Harbour Lights*, 1885

Plate 10. W. L. Abingdon by Max Beerbohm

Plate 11. *The Girl I Left Behind Me*, 1895

Plate 12. *One of the Best*, 1895

Plate 13. Private entrance, Adelphi Theatre, 1897

Plate 14. Scene from *The Union Jack*, 1888

Plate 15. Richard Archer Prince in 1897

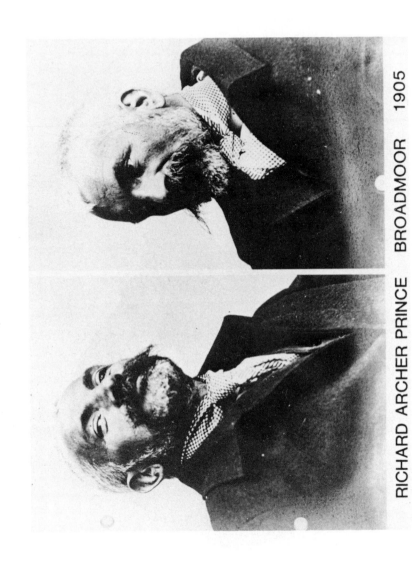

RICHARD ARCHER PRINCE   BROADMOOR   1905

Plate 16. Richard Archer Prince in 1905

Faced by such behaviour, it says much for Elliston's tolerance that he continued to employ Prince over four or five seasons. Nevertheless his stock declined. By the end of the 1894–5 tour, he was, according to Percival, "*very* hard up and the company 'subbed' to pay his fare to London". Their charity seems to have proved vain, for there was no work going either in London or the provinces, and the humiliated actor was forced to return to Dundee and his family.

The next few months are fully if wretchedly documented. Prince obtained employment in an ironworks and "was a good worker", according to the foreman, David Simpson, when called at the trial,[12] but his conduct outside the foundry left everything to be desired. His mother admitted he had "turns", and his eyes would "stare out of his head".[13] He complained that his food and drink were being poisoned. He attacked his brother, Harry, with a knife (ominous again) and "put his mother outside the door, and they had to go to a neighbour's house".[14] On occasions he would claim to be "a second Jesus Christ".[15]

His theatrical ambitions remained. He frequently visited Her Majesty's, where he would "present an envelope bearing in writing 'Mr. Richard A. Prince from the Adelphi Theatre, London'", and claim a seat in the best part of the house. But his dress and conduct proved an embarrassment to the management. He would wear "a tall hat, a velvet jacket, and sometimes a white vest and tri-coloured sash". He tended to "applaud the artists when there was no call to do so, and occasionally endeavour to enter into a conversation with them from his seat in the body of the house".[6] After the murder "a theatrical official" (perhaps the Robert Beveridge who gave evidence at the trial) told the *Dundee Advertiser* of "having eventually to carry him from the dress-circle and expel him from the building" because Prince had uttered threats to shoot one of the actors, and had brandished a revolver.[17]

Above all the prodigal son spoke of malice from many theatrical figures who had blocked his professional progress. He accused numerous managers of "blackmailing" him (presumably "blackballing" was meant), the list including Elliston, Robert Arthur, lessee of Her Majesty's, and inevitably Terriss. Elliston later spoke of blood-curdling threats in a letter which ran:

You hell-hound. You Judas. You have got me out of engagements
by blackmailing me to get on yourself. You cur. I am not a woman.
You hound, how dare you blackmail a Highlander? Next time I ask
you for a reference, it will be at Bow Street Police Station, where
my lawyer will expose you. If I die at Newgate, you will be to blame.
I would advise you to take this letter to Scotland Yard this time.
Victory or death is my motto, and the fear of God.

I am,

RICHARD ARTHUR (*sic*) PRINCE[18]

If only Elliston had followed this advice!

By the end of 1895 Prince had exhausted Dundee's patience.
"To put it shortly, he has been a perpetual nuisance", commented
the theatre official later, "and we were not sorry when he left
again for London."[19] There he made contact with the sister who
had been instrumental in his going to London originally. Now
began an episode of which not one word was spoken at the trial,
nor a whisper leaked to the press, yet which led directly to disaster.
Such evidence as survives rests largely on the testimony of Seymour Hicks, writing thirty years later in *Between Ourselves*, by
which time in his words "there is no reason why the true story
of William Terriss's end should not now be told". Without corroboration, the story calls for caution. On the other hand Hicks,
both as the victim's son-in-law and co-author of the play which
provided the background to the episode, commands personal and
professional authority.

His account refers to a member of the Adelphi company who

> was on intimate terms with a female relative of the man Prince, a
> woman well known to be a frequenter of the then notorious Empire
> promenade.

The promenade at the Empire Theatre, Leicester Square, was
much patronised in the 1890s by prostitutes and their clients. In
1894 a move to partition it off was vigorously opposed, one of
the leading opponents being Winston Churchill, then a Sandhurst
cadet. Hick's description of "Mrs. Archer" continues:

> She was by no means an unattractive specimen of her class, and it
> is certain that this lady of uneasy virtue was the means of her brother,

Prince, becoming known to her admirer, who acceded to her request that he should help her relative to earn a living in the theatre.[20]

This member of the Adelphi company is identified by Hicks as "Mr. A.", and described as "a capital actor and a pleasant enough companion, though by no means possessed of any particularly attractive qualities".[21] He was in fact W. L. (another William) Abingdon, who had joined the company during the run of *The Silver Falls* seven years before, and been chiefly employed at the Adelphi ever since. In *One of the Best* (the piece Hicks had written with George Edwardes) he played the villainous Squire Ellsworth to Terriss's Dudley Keppel; he was almost always cast as the villain, and Hicks transposes their stage-relationship to real life:

> Outwardly to Terriss, "Mr. A." was agreeable and hail-fellow-well-met, but behind his back he never lost an opportunity of belittling the man who, being himself of the most frank and charming disposition, was quite unconscious of the venom which lurked behind the smile of the man he looked upon as a good comrade.[22]

There was certainly a streak of misanthropy in Abingdon's make-up. On the one occasion he was not cast as an Adelphi villain (in a revival of *The Shaughraun*) he was judged a failure, and he may well have begrudged Terriss his looks, breeding, and swift rise to success. In his entry in *The Green Room Book* Abingdon wrote: "At the end of the season [1881] he found himself 'out', and for the subsequent two years he roughed it in all parts of the provinces". One of the few performances in London he gave outside the Adelphi and Princess's (both seats of melodrama) was ominously portentous: in the English premiere of Zola's *Thérèse Raquin* (staged by the avant-garde Independent Theatre) he played Laurent, the lover who helps Thérèse to murder her husband, and ultimately carries out a suicide pact when the accusing gaze of Madame Raquin destroys their nerve. Much the same could be said of Abingdon's own end.

There is no mention of Prince in the playbill for *One of the Best*, but there was nothing new about such an omission. What is surprising is Hicks's assertion that

> To please Prince, "Mr. A." had the part of the hero, the part Terriss was playing, typed for him to learn, and indeed went so far as to

65

have what to him was a comic rehearsal called, and with the assistance of the extra people in the piece, had a hilarious hour watching the miserable weakling make a complete jackass of himself.[23]

It seems unthinkable that Prince should have been allotted the task of understudying Terriss. More likely, since *One of the Best* opened on 21 December 1895, there was some sort of Christmas party, with Abingdon as Lord of Misrule, at which the current piece was burlesqued, and Prince allowed to play (though unwittingly) a travesty Dudley Keppel. Reversion to his Scots brogue would have commended such casting, since Keppel is an officer in the 42nd Highlanders. It seems extraordinary, however, that even so unbalanced a creature should have been unaware of his fellow-actors' contempt, although Hicks specifically states:

> Prince's fellow-supers, with whom he dressed, little realizing on what thin ice they were travelling, encouraged him for their amusement to talk more grandiloquently than ever of what he would do, should his great day ever arrive.[24]

On the other hand the management was evidently unimpressed, for Prince was not re-engaged once the run of *One of the Best* finished. Hicks's explanation – "there being comparatively few supers needed for the play which followed mine"[25] – is presumably a white lie: the piece in question, *Boys Together*, contained elaborate crowd and battle scenes in Egypt and the Sudan, to which Prince's "foreign" accent would have lent verisimilitude.

By the summer of 1896 his plight was desperate. Out of work and (if Abingdon had been unable or unwilling to protect him at the Adelphi) alienated from his sister, he seemed to have reached the end of the line, and the story circulating at the time of his trial that he had earlier attempted suicide by jumping into the Regent's Canal may well relate to this crisis.[26] At any rate he turned up once more in Dundee, to the alarm of his family and former associates. He does not appear to have plagued the theatre with his presence – he had little to boast of and much to conceal – but the incident related by a neighbour, Andrew Moffatt, that Prince "had sung from 7 o'clock in the evening to 1 o'clock in the morning" seems to refer to this visitation.[27] On the other hand he had no difficulty in obtaining work at the Wallace

Foundry, where the foreman, Alexander Husband, later deposed he "did his work satisfactorily" and "left the foundry of his own accord to join a theatrical company".[28]

The company in question was that of Arthur Carlton, a third-rate manager from the Crown Theatre, Stoke-on-Trent. In the summer of 1897 he had sent out a tour of *The Union Jack* (a flag which seems scarcely ever to have been struck on the provincial stage in the 1890s). Even so, Prince's reputation in his home town ought to have discouraged his further employment in the theatre. It appears, however, that Carlton's company ran into serious casting difficulties while playing the Grand Theatre, Glasgow, and Prince's availability and knowledge of the piece may have seemed a solution. The company's stage-manager, Douglas Phelps, later confirmed that in an emergency Prince was recruited to play the part of the chief villain, Sir Philip Yorke.[29]

This casting was horribly prophetic. Yorke, although the author of most of the disasters in the play, is himself being blackmailed by Captain Morton who knows him to be a forger. The climax of Yorke's part (the last and probably the longest that the wretched Prince ever played) runs:

MORTON   (*seeing the knife*) What have you there?

YORKE   Give me that bill!

MORTON   Madman! (*gripping YORKE*)

YORKE   (*lifting the knife*) By Heaven, I'll have it or I'll murder you! Give it to me!

MORTON   No. (*struggle – YORKE stabs him*)

          (*Reenter ETHEL through curtains as CAPT. MORTON falls – YORKE kneels over him, searching – ETHEL horror-stricken*)

The effect of this scene on Prince's mind, already crazed with an imaginary grievance against Terriss, may be deduced. By October the management had discovered that, far from resolving their difficulty by employing Prince, they had created another and bigger. When the company reached South Shields, he was dismissed, on the grounds (according to him) that he "smoked a clay pipe instead of a cigar".[30] This may reflect some part of the alleged grounds for dismissal – that he could not represent convincingly a titled Colonel – but the truth was his mind had deteriorated so far, he could no longer retain lines or sustain any part.

This truth another manager, Ralph Croydon, at that moment recruiting another company in Newcastle and on his own evidence "in a fix", did not guess. Croydon's professional standing was even less exalted than Carlton's – he ran what amounted to a "fit-up" company, playing mostly one-night stands in Northumberland and Durham – and Princes's mental decline at this time is reflected in his descent from Elliston's management to Carlton's and now to Croydon's. But reassured by Prince's references to the Adelphi and touring in *The Union Jack*, the harassed manager interviewed him at the Amphitheatre, Newcastle, on 23 October, and signed him to play Sir Lester Lightfoot in *Nurse Charity* and Sir Geoffrey Dashwood in *Parson Thorn*.[31] The trappings of these roles are impressive; their importance was apparently slight, and the degree of Croydon's need was great.

So began Prince's last, briefest, and best-documented engagement. The next day being Sunday, Mrs. Croydon invited him to tea at their Newcastle home. If the idea was to make the parties better acquainted, the invitation failed in its object. Prince struck attitudes, declaiming: "His foot was on his native heath; his name it was MacGregor" (a favourite tag from saner days) and adding, with reference to his departure from the *Union Jack* company: "My name's MacGregor, but I'll smoke a clay-pipe if I like." Seeking to lighten the atmosphere, the lady passed round an illustrated magazine, and it was on this occasion that Prince identified a beauty wearing a powdered wig and brocade gown as his sister, pointing to his own grey hairs and adding: "It's only this secret sorrow that's made me what I am."[32]

Croydon's company was due to open at the small mining town of Hetton two days later, and had a "train-call" next morning. Prince caught the train but refused to travel with his colleagues. Summoned to rehearsal, his incapacity became increasingly apparent. He could scarcely remember one of his lines, "rolled his eyes in a wild fashion, and pressed his temples". When a break was tactfully called and one of the company produced a knife

to open a tin of sardines, the recruit asked that it be put away
as he did not like the look of it. Later, however, he picked up
a "property" dagger and observed: "A man would not want that
stuck in many times." Before the day was out Croydon had accepted the inevitable and dismissed his recent signing, whereupon
Prince proposed the Tuesday performance be cancelled to give
him more time. When Croydon refused, he exclaimed:

"I have now got two enemies: one here, one at the Adelphi."

When Croydon remonstrated, emphasising the respect in which
Terriss was held, the disgraced actor replied:

"Fools often succeed where men of genius fail."

Nevertheless, the man of genius turned up no less than five times
next day at Croydon's lodgings, begging for his wages. After the
manager finally dismissed him as a madman, he retorted:

"Mad? Mad? You will hear of my madness.
The whole world will ring with it."[33]

On this grimly prophetic note he abandoned Croydon, the company, and his home territory, and make his way to London by
sea. There are suggestions that in the 1880s, between theatrical
engagements, he had served as a ship's steward as well as valet,[34]
and perhaps he still had some connections on the boats. Evidently
he could not find his fare, for in December after his arrest he
stated that his theatrical "skip" was still lying at Trades Wharf,
Wapping, as a pledge.[35] But he had reached London by 28
October, and on that day found a room at 3/- a week with Mrs.
Charlotte Darby in Eaton Court, Buckingham Palace Road.[36]

One of his first outings was to the cutler's establishment of
Mr. George Lorberg in Brompton Road, where his peculiar dress
and manner impressed themselves on the proprietor's memory,
so that he recalled "a tall, shabbily-dressed man" answering to
Prince's description buying a knife for 9d one evening at the end
of October. The shopkeeper pressed a superior article at 1/- on
him, but the customer could not afford it.[37]

Another outing was to the Adelphi. The stage-doorkeeper,
Henry Spratt, remembered Prince calling on 9 November and

asking for a note to be sent up to Terriss, from whom a reply was forthcoming. This reply, in the form of a reference for the Actors' Benevolent Fund, was later produced in evidence, and ran:

"I have known the bearer, R. A. Prince, as a hard-working actor."[38]

It was a tribute, not to the obscure "super" but to the fatally generous leading man.

For the next six weeks Prince made frequent requests for financial assistance to the Fund. His begging letters were produced at the trial, and make melancholy reading:

To the Gentlemen of the Committee:
Gentlemen,
   The reason I have to ask for help is that I was out of an engagement for over 12 months before I received the last one, and lost it through no fault of my own. All the time I was in my last engagement, I had to spend all my money in dressing the parts of Captain Morton and Sir Philip Yorke. When I left off on Saturday night I had not a shilling to call my own. I have parted with everything I have in the world. My box is at the dock for my fare and passage. I have nowhere else to go. I thought I might get something to do in town. For the last six or seven years all the engagements I have had, it has taken the money I received from them to keep me on tour. It was taking me all my time to live without being able to save. If you will only help me to live for a week or two, I think I shall be able to get an engagement.

Yours faithfully

RICHARD A. PRINCE[39]

This plea produced a contribution of £1. Prince also stated that his sister gave him £1, implying that she declined any further assistance. Probably the Abingdon affair still divided them, and she may also have marked the deterioration in his mental state. Before long he was applying again to the Secretary of the Benevolent Fund:

Dear Sir,
   Last week I was too ill to go home. Besides, I thought I would get an engagement for South Africa. I enclose letter, and I stood a chance of another engagement at Woolwich, *Under Remand*

company. Was down last Friday at Woolwich, and saw manager, but
it's not settled. I missed the bus, and had to walk home eight miles
on Saturday. I was quite done up. Besides, I didn't know I had a
home to go to until Tuesday. I enclose letter from my little sister.
You will see for yourself I am not a liar. If the gentlemen of the
Actor's Benevolent Fund does (*sic*) not help me another once I shall
have to starve or die. I have done everything I know to get an
engagement, and been to all the gentlemen in London to get me one,
but have settled nothing yet. If you will kindly put my sad case before
the gentlemen of the committee once more, I shall abide by their
decision. Thanking you all for your great kindness,

Yours faithfully

R. ARCHER PRINCE[40]

With a mind as confused as Prince's it is impossible to decide
how serious was his search for work. He certainly made contact
with R. St. John Denton, the actor he had dressed with in *Harbour
Lights* and now a theatrical agent, who reported his coming to
his office "in a deplorable state". Denton did what he could, fixing
him up for a pantomime chorus, only to learn he had been turned
down "because of the cast in his eye". He also obtained for him
the part of Lord Mountsevern "in a small production of *East
Lynne*", but this too was withdrawn because "he had no frock-
coat".[41]

By the end of November Prince's appeals to the Committee
sounded increasingly forlorn:

Dear Sir,
     I shall not get an engagement in London now. You might ask the
gentlemen of the committee if they would kindly lend me a pound
to take me home. The ship goes today. After they have been so kind,
they might do this if you will ask. Thanking you for your kindness,

Yours faithfully

R. ARCHER PRINCE

In all the Committee made him four payments, of £1, £1, 10/-
and 10/-.[42]

At Eaton Place Mrs. Darby seems to have been unaware of
her lodger's mental condition. In evidence she insisted "the prisoner was cheerful while in her house and conducted himself like

a gentleman". She could hardly fail to observe the change in his physical condition. In her own words: "I noticed that his clothing was gradually disappearing. He bought his own food."[43] In fact he lived on a diet of bread and milk, and divided his time between lying in bed and writing letters, Correspondence had long been one of his obsessions: when his room was searched after the murder, acknowledgements were discovered from the Duke and Duchess of York (for a poem on the birth of the future King Edward VIII), from Princess Beatrice (for condolences on the death of her husband, Prince Henry of Battenburg), and Mr. Gladstone (occasion unspecified).[44]

Some of the letters he wrote from Eaton Court would have surprised his landlady and should have spurred the police into action. The resemblance in the names of Terry and Terriss seems to have singled out Fred Terry and his wife, Julia Neilson, for special treatment, particularly when they turned down a play, *Countess Otho*, which Prince had written. Fred Terry was rebuked:

> Sir,
>   Please return play *Countess Otho* at once. If you are hard up for the money will send it. Terriss, the Pope, Scotland Yard. I will answer in a week.

and Julia Neilson received the following:

> Madam,
>   I thank you as a Highlander and a gentleman, in the name of the Almighty God, our Queen, and my rights for play *Countess Otho*.[45]

In view of the widely circulated story that Prince murdered William Terriss in mistake for another actor, Edward Terry, whom he believed to have turned down his final plea to the Actors' Benevolent Fund, it should be emphasised that Terriss had been the object of his spleen for some ten years, and that by this point Prince's mind had become obsessed with hatred of most leading actors, particularly those with names like Terriss or Terry.

During these weeks Prince made repeated visits to the Adelphi stage-door, where he was recognised by his strange dress as the "mad Archer" who had walked on years before. Testimony to his appearance abounded: by this time the evening clothes and coloured sash were probably in the pawnbroker's keeping, but all the accounts stress the slouch hat and long cape, several pointing out his resemblance in both dress and looks to the traditional stage-villain. It must have been his long-standing status as "mad Archer" and his melodramatic appearance and manner that allowed so many of his acquaintances to treat him as a harmless eccentric. Their contemptuous dismissal was understandable – but fatal.

By the beginning of December Prince's funds were clearly exhausted. He owed Mrs Darby two weeks' rent and asked for a few days' grace. When this ran out, he admitted he had no money, adding "what shall I do?" Her response was: "I don't know, Mr. Prince. I am sorry for you." He still had hopes, he told her, of help from his sister, after which "It would be one way or the other." When she asked what he meant, he replied: "That is best known to God or man."[46]

On the evening of 15 December he made another visit to the stage-door of the Adelphi and asked Spratt, the doorkeeper, if Terriss would shortly come that way. Spratt was well aware that the star and one or two other members of the company used the private entrance in Maiden Lane installed for Queen Victoria and the Prince Consort when they patronised the theatre incognito. Sensing trouble, however, he replied that Terriss did use the stage-door but would not give interviews. According to one account "mad Archer" murmured "Not yet" and turned away.[47]

Next day he asked his landlady for some hot water but was refused. He left the house, and his movements for the remainder of the day can be reconstructed in outline. A final visit to the office of the Actors' Benevolent Fund proved vain. He was refused access to the Secretary, and referred to a clerk, who told him his last application had been considered by the Committee and rejected. He "turned round and left the room without saying anything".[48] Prince next made his way to the office of the agent, St. John Denton, in Maiden Lane, to ask if any work was available. Again he was turned down.

It was still too early to pester the stage-doorkeeper at the Adelphi, but the desperate man walked a few yards into the Strand.

And here occurred a final catastrophic encounter. Prince came face to face with his sister, on the arm, in his words, of "her husband" (presumably a client from the Empire Promenade; perhaps even Abingdon himself). He made another appeal for money and "she said she would rather see me dead in the gutter than give me a farthing".[49]

He turned back to Maiden Lane and placed himself opposite the Adelphi private entrance.

Notes

1   *Times* 14 January 1898
2   *Ibid.*
3   *Dundee Advertiser* 20 December 1897
4   *Era* 18 December 1897
5   *Dundee Advertiser* 22 December 1897
6   *Ibid.*
7   *My Life* p. 270
8   *Dundee People's Journal* 25 December 1897
9   *Dundee Advertiser* 20 December 1897
10 *Times* 14 January 1898
11 *Dundee People's Journal* 25 December 1897
12 *Times* 14 January 1898
13 *Ibid.*
14 *Ibid.*
15 *Dundee Courier* 18 December 1897
16 *Dundee Advertiser* 18 December 1897
17 *Ibid.*
18 *Dundee Advertiser* 20 December 1897
19 *Dundee Advertiser* 18 December 1897
20 Seymour Hicks: *Between Ourselves* (London, Cassell, 1930) p. 36
21 *Ibid.* p. 37
22 *Ibid.*
23 *Ibid.* pp. 37/38
24 *Ibid.* p. 39
25 *Ibid.*
26 *Dundee Advertiser* 20 December 1897
27 *Times* 14 January 1898
28 *Ibid.*
29 *Dundee Advertiser* 22 December 1897

74

30 *Dundee Advertiser* 20 December 1897
31 *Ibid.*
32 *Ibid.*
33 *Ibid.*
34 *Dundee Advertiser* 18 December 1897
35 *Dundee Advertiser* 27 December 1897
36 *Times* 14 January 1898
37 *Ibid.*
38 *Dundee Advertiser* 30 December 1897
39 *Times* 14 January 1898
40 *Ibid.*
41 *Dundee Advertiser* 22 December 1897
42 *Times* 14 January 1898
43 *Ibid.*
44 *Ibid.*
45 *Dundee Advertiser* 20 December 1897
46 *Times* 23 December 1897
47 *Times* 17 December 1897
48 *Dundee Courier* 18 December 1897
49 *Times* 21 December 1897

V: The Sensation Scene

Dramatic theorists are given to distinguishing between tragedy and melodrama by contrasting the function in each of the catastrophe or climax. In tragedy, they maintain, it is inherent from the start, usually through the fatal flaw of the protagonist. As a modern French practitioner has put it: "The spring is wound up tight. It will unwind of itself."[1] In melodrama, on the other hand, the denouement is superimposed for theatrical effect; the greater the surprise, the more stunning the impact. On such an analysis the death of William Terriss lacked tragic inevitability, so much so that eye-witnesses and public alike could not believe it had happened. As the climax of a melodrama, however, it fell short of the spectacular dimension such scenes provided. The narrow confines of Maiden Lane, and the handful of participants, principals and onlookers, were wretched substitutes for battle-fields, storm-tossed seas or burning buildings.

Prince's assault was so swift that only the victim realised what had happened. The key-witness, John Henry Graves, who had not only known Terriss all his life but had signed the register at his wedding, related at the trial how the two men caught a cab from Jessie Millward's flat, arriving outside the Adelphi private entrance at a few minutes after seven. Terriss called: "Wait a minute, Harry, till I get my key." As he bent down to open the door, Prince rushed across the road and dealt him two blows in the back which poor Graves "first thought were in friendship". As the actor turned round, his killer struck him a third time. Only when Terriss cried out: "My God! I am stabbed!" did his

76

companion realise the truth.[2] Graves had no difficulty (but showed great courage) in holding Prince until a constable appeared. There were cries of "Murder" and "Police" from the bystanders (estimated at between three and twelve by different witnesses). These cries were heard by Police Constable Bragg from Bow Street station, who was on duty in the vicinity, and who took Prince into custody on Graves's accusation. After giving his evidence to Inspector French at Bow Street, Graves returned to the Adelphi to do his last service for his old friend.

Accounts of Terriss's dying moments are understandably more confused than those of the attack. There were more witnesses and the atmosphere was charged with panic and horror. It is clear that the actor's wounds were too severe to allow him even to be carried upstairs to his dressing-room. Jessie was mercifully spared giving evidence at the trial and her account dates from twenty-five years later. She dashed downstairs and found Terriss leaning against the wall, just inside the private entrance.

"Sis", he said faintly, "Sis, I am stabbed!"
I put my arms round him to support him, when we both fell to the ground on the bare boards at the foot of the stairs leading to our dressing-rooms.

Medical help was summoned from Charing Cross Hospital, in particular that of the senior housesurgeon, a Mr. Hayward, who realised that the blow to the heart, given when Terriss turned round to face his assailant, was fatal. Soon the medical men and doubtless some of the theatre staff were joined by Inspector French from Bow Street. The end came a few minutes before eight. Jessie recalled the moment in the following words:

He was lying on my right arm, and I held his hand in my left hand.
We were now alone.
He opened his eyes, and faintly squeezed my hand.
"Sis! Sis!" he whispered.
And that was all.[3]

The two members of the Terriss family readily available were Tom Terriss and Seymour Hicks. For Hicks the moment was already one of sadness and strain. Only two weeks before Ellaline had lost her first child, a boy, and was still not recovered. Her husband had returned to the cast of *The Circus Girl* in which both had been appearing at the Gaiety. Unconscious of the events only a few hundred yards away, Hicks had dressed and made up for his part, only to be told by the stage-manager, to whom the murder had been reported, that his understudy would be playing. Instead he was summoned (unnecessarily, it would seem) to Bow Street to identify Prince, whom he describes as "a savage animal . . . foaming at the mouth".[4]

From there he hurried to the Adelphi, where the stage-manager, Fred Latham, escorted him to Terriss's dressing-room, in which the dead man's body now lay. Hicks's terror was at once allayed by the calm on Terriss's face and what he describes as "the smile upon his lips". Years later he was to write:

> In the serenity and quiet of that room I to this day feel sure I heard a voice say to me, "Are there men living such fools as to think there is no hereafter?"
> That night I knew beyond all shadow of doubt that William Terriss and myself would meet again.[5]

Meanwhile Hicks's dresser, Fred, had been sent to Bedford Park, where Tom Terriss, now twenty-five and making headway as an actor, had returned from rehearsal. Fred accompanied him back to the Adelphi, but apparently the poor man either dared not or could not bring himself to break the news. In notes for an unfinished autobiography Tom Terriss records:

> When they get off the train at Charing Cross Tom hears a newsboy shouting something about a murder but misses most of the cry, and they go on to the theatre in a cab. There at the stage-door is Harry Nicholls. He breaks the news to Tom that his father has been murdered, stabbed by a demented stage-hand. He takes Tom into Bill Terriss's dressing-room, where Father is laid on an improvised bier. Tom doesn't really take it all in until he touches his father's forehead, which is as cold as marble. He faints.[6]

In a theatrical world as concentrated as that of the 1890s news of Terriss's murder spread instantly. Budd, the Adelphi manager, had the distressing task of announcing to the assembled audience:

> Ladies and gentlemen, I an deeply grieved and pained to announce to you a serious, nay terrible, accident which will render the perfor-

mance of *Secret Service* this evening quite impossible. I will also ask you to pass out into the street as quietly as possible. It is hardly necessary for me to add that your money will be returned on application at the pay-boxes.[7]

All along the Strand other companies received the news with incredulity, or where believed, anger and a personal grief. Perhaps the most moving of the many stories told of that night is related by Johnston Forbes-Robertson, who was playing Hamlet at the Lyceum, where fifteen years before he had played Claudio with Terriss as Don Pedro beside him. Here the company, marshalled by Ian Robertson, the actor's brother, made a pact to keep the news from their leader until after the performance, and although aware of a strange silence backstage, he descended from his dressing-room to make his entrance ignorant of the reason. But in the wings he noticed a stage-hand in unconcealable tears, and asking the cause, heard the poor man blurt out:

Oh, sir, Mr. Terriss is murdered![8]

The funeral took place five days later at Brompton Cemetery, and was preceded by a service at the Chapel Royal of the Savoy, only a few yards away from the Adelphi. The intense grief felt by a public whose personal knowledge of any actor must have been severely restricted in the days before the universal exposure imposed by the film, had already been apparent in the Press coverage of the murder, but was even more visible in the crowds lining the route and filling the Cemetery. The *Times* estimated their number at 50,000.[9] The list of those who sent flowers included almost every leading theatre name of the day, and, less predictably, was headed by the Prince of Wales. Royal recognition of the actor's profession was still rare; Irving's knighthood had been conferred only two years earlier, and Bancroft's that summer.

Much comment has focussed on Jessie Millward's presence at the funeral, to which she was escorted by Irving and Seymour Hicks. It is an accepted tenet of theatrical lore that Irving's gesture in accompanying Jessie was made to protect her from the malice of theatrical gossip and the resentment of the Terriss family. There is, however, a simpler explanation for her request and his generous response. Victorian funerals were essentially male occasions, which even the closest female relatives did not usually attend. The official list of mourners at Terriss's includes only two other women: a Mrs. Iredell (with her husband, Major Iredell) and Madame Antoinette Sterling. Any suggestion of resentment by the Terriss family is rebuffed by the additional protection of Terriss's son-in-law, Seymour Hicks. It is overwhelmingly clear that Jessie had been and remained the closest of friends with Ellaline and her husband, as Ellaline's letter to her, already quoted, underlines.

In the published version of *Myself and Others* Jessie's account of Irving's offer includes this passage:

> One afternoon my sister came to me.
> "Sir Henry Irving is here to see you", she said.
> "Please don't refuse; he has a message for you."
> "I will see him", I replied, and he came into my room.
> "My dear", he said, "I have just come from Bedford Park. I was asked to convey to the Terriss family a message of condolence from the Queen, and I felt that I must come to you to tell you how we all sympathize with you."
> Then he went on to tell me that the Prince of Wales had sent his equerry with a message of sympathy for me.
> "Is there anything else I can do for you?" he asked gently.
> "Yes", I answered; "I should like you to be with me at the funeral."
> "Of course, my dear", he replied.
> Every night after his performance of "Peter the Great" he came to sit an hour with me, talking of the theatre, of art, and work, and endeavouring, as I afterwards realized, to keep alive in me some interest in my profession and my life-work.
> All the Monday night my brother Frank and Seymour Hicks sat by my bedside, and next morning, punctually at half past ten, Sir Henry Irving called, bearing in his hands a large bunch of violets. He, Seymour and I drove to Brompton together . . .[10]

Jessie's manuscript, however, has slight but significant variations:

> He then asked if there anything he could do for me.
> I said: "Yes, I should like you to take me to the funeral on Tuesday."
> He said "Certainly".
> Every night after his performance of "Peter the Great" by his son Laurence he came and spent an hour with me and talked about the

80

theatre. I knew he was in the habit after the performance to entertain friends at supper in his rooms at the Lyceum or go straight to the Garrick Club. Outside my own family and the Terriss family I did not want to see anyone. On the Monday night my brother Frank and Seymour Hicks sat by my bedside . . .[11]

The sentence: "Outside my own family and the Terriss family I did not want to see anyone", omitted in the published account, casts a different light on Jessie's position, though Irving's generosity is in no way diminished.

In complete contrast to the scale and intense feeling of the funeral, the inquest on 20 December was brief and formal. There was no doubt how Terriss had died, or who had killed him. On the other hand Prince's trial before Mr. Justice Channel on 13 January examined at some length the question: why was he killed? C. F. Gill and Horace Avery, appearing for the prosecution, called a wide range of witnesses. Tom Terriss (identified as "Thomas Lewin, actor") spoke for the family. Poor Henry Graves repeated the details of the actual killing he had already given at the inquest, and no less than four police inspectors followed up the story. Other witnesses filled in Prince's bleak theatrical background: Denton, agent and former colleague; Henry Spratt, the Adelphi stagedoor-keeper, and William Algar, Terriss's dresser; Ralph Croydon, from Newcastle, Prince's last employer. Two spokesmen from the Actors' Benevolent Fund, C. E. Colson and A. H. Holland, confirmed the desperate straits which prompted Prince's appeals to them, and his landlady, Charlotte Darby, completed their account. A surprise witness, who must have come forward in response to the police's appeal, was George Lorberg, the cutler who sold Prince the fatal knife two months earlier.

When Messrs. Sands and Kyd opened the case for the defence, their questions were put mostly to Prince's family and associates from Dundee. Mother, sister Maggie, and brother Harry all elaborated on the prisoner's blighted childhood. Two former workmates, Alexander Husband and David Simpson, spoke as loyally as they could, without concealing Prince's aberrations. Elliston, his manager from Lancashire, and Robert Beveridge of Her Majesty's Theatre, Dundee, agreed that he had presented them with insuperable problems. No less than three medical men from

Holloway, Doctors Bastian, Hyslop and Scott, underlined his mental instability, and Doctor Fitch, superintendent of a lunatic asylum at Salisbury, confirmed the circumstances of James Archer's (presumably a step-brother) death.

A witness conspicuously absent was "Mrs. Archer". Instead Mary Waller, "a servant in the employ of Mrs. Archer", testified that the prisoner was in the habit of calling at the house, and that she "had heard he was Mrs. Archer's step-brother". He had visited the house six times in November and December, but not for a fortnight or so before the murder.[12]

Evidently "Mrs. Archer" had found it prudent to disappear. Her shadowy responsibility for William Abingdon's part in encouraging Prince's *folie de grandeur* is lent some credence by Seymour Hicks's story that on the morning after the funeral two stalwarts of the Adelphi company, James Beveridge and Charles Somerset, confronted Abingdon, "telling him that they laid their friend's death at his door", whereupon "he completely broke down".[13] In fact Abingdon left the Adelphi after the run of *Boys Together* and had been appearing at other London theatres. His subsequent career was significant: amongst his West End roles were Judge Jeffreys in *Sweet Nell of Old Drury* and Professor Moriarty to the Sherlock Holmes of William Gillette, both black-blooded villains. But in 1903 he moved his scene of operations to America, where his fortunes, at first prospering, came to a disastrous conclusion, as will be shown.

There was no difficulty for Mr. Justice Channel in summing up:

> Having referred to the evidence and to the testimony of the medical experts, who had expressed the unanimous and undoubted opinion that the prisoner was insane, the learned Judge concluded by observing that the questions were, first, whether the jury were satisfied that the prisoner committed the act and, secondly, whether it had been made to appear to them that, at the time he committed it, he was not responsible, according to law, by reason of disease of the mind.[14]

The jury retired for half an hour, returned and found the prisoner Guilty of wilful murder, but on the medical evidence not responsible for his actions. When the Judge ordered the prisoner to be detained as a criminal lunatic at Holloway until Her

Majesty's pleasure be known, something of the actor stirred in Prince who then broke out:

> Shall I not be allowed to make a statement of thanks to the Court? I should like to thank all the gentlemen who have assisted in the case. I did not bring my defence properly forward after the medical evidence because I did not think it necessary, and because I should not have been believed. All that I can say is that I have had a very fair trial and that –
> MR. JUSTICE CHANNEL: I cannot allow any statement now. It is better not.
> THE PRISONER: All I can say is that I thank you.
> MR. JUSTICE CHANNEL: You are entitled to thank your counsel.[15]

After the legal ceremonial and argument of the trial, there is a touching simplicity about Tom Terriss's postscript to the tragedy. His mother had been in poor health before the murder, and no doubt this, following the grave illness of Ellaline and the loss of a grandchild, devastated her. The notes for an autobiography read:

> Later that winter, along towards the end of it, Tom goes with his Mother to Algeria, realizing she is not in very good health ... Upon returning from Algeria, Tom's Mother dies within a few months – during the summer of that year.[16]

Poor "Izzie" had lost the will to survive her partner.

Notes

1 Jean Anouilh: *Antigone* translated by Lewis Galantière (London, Methuen, 1951) p. 34.
2 *Times* 14 January 1898.
3 Millward p. 231.
4 *Between Ourselves* pp. 41–3.
5 *ibid*. p. 43.
6 Chapter X p. 4.
7 *Daily Telegraph* 17 December 1897.
8 Johnston Forbes-Robertson: *A Player under Three Reigns* (London, Fisher Unwin, 1925) pp. 117–18.
9 *Times* 22 December 1897.

10 Millward pp. 233–4
11 I am indebted to Professor James Ellis of Mount Holyoke College, U.S.A.,
    the present owner, for permission to quote from this MS.
12 *Times* 14 January 1898.
13 *Between Ourselves* p. 44.
14 *Times* 14 January 1898.
15 *ibid.*
16 Chapter X pp. 4–5.

VI: The Epilogue

The final item which Terriss's devoted sister Harriet pasted into the scrapbook she had kept throughout his career is a cutting, dated September 1903, telling of a "smart" young lady, hitherto impervious to any actor's appeal, who left the Adelphi "a veritable Niobe" after seeing *Black-Eye'd Susan*. The grieving sister has added:

> Written six years after his death, so he is still remembered by some, although he always said a few months would be the length of time for remembrance.[1]

Terriss's comment chimes in with his favourite tags, "Carpe diem" and "Tempus fugit", especially as elaborated by Gordon Craig to

> All applause is mockery, and the noise has scarce died away when those who make it and those for whom it is given are *forgotten*.[2]

Nevertheless there was no danger of Terriss being forgotten in the years immediately following his death. Inevitably much of what was written was charged with emotion, and the actor's admirers had to prize the sentiment while pardoning the sentimentality of this tribute to him in *Punch*:

> "Shadows we are, and shadows we pursue",
> That was the motto dearest far to you!
> Old friend and comrade, having grasped my hand,
> I mourn you lost to me in Shadow Land.

85

Brave Sailor Lad! and best of "pals" on earth,
Whose triumph at your death, proclaimed your worth,
They bore you down an avenue of woe,
Where men and women sobbed, "We loved him so!"

Why did they love him? The assassin's knife,
With one fell blow, mangled a loyal life,
They loved him for his honour! Splendid Will!
That made a hero of our "BREEZY BILL!"[3]

A more apt tribute arose on the Grand Parade at Eastbourne in the form of a new Lifeboat House, built from contributions to a memorial fund organised by the *Daily Telegraph*. There was a double fitness in the choice. Not only was Terriss himself a skilled sailor who had saved others from drowning; shortly before his death he had sponsored an appeal, also in the *Telegraph*, for a memorial to the victims of a lifeboat disaster at Margate, where he had himself sailed and swum throughout his life.

The foundation stone of the Terriss Memorial at Eastbourne was laid by the Duchess of Devonshire on 16 July 1898. In his address Charles Wyndham spoke feelingly:

What he was before the public he was to his friends in private. Every heroic deed of his upon the stage was just such as we could imagine him performing off the boards – nay, as on more than one occasion he did perform. It is impossible to conceive a grander parallel between the artist and the man. He lived a life as worthy and died a death as tragic as any man he had represented on the stage.[4]

More permanent was the inscription which the building still bears:

This Life-boat House has been erected in memory of WILLIAM TERRISS with subscriptions received by the "DAILY TELE-GRAPH" from those who loved and admired him, and who sorrowed together with all his friends and fellow countrymen at his most untimely end.

1898
"Shadows we are and shadows we pursue."

another reminder of Terriss's inbred modesty.

A second memorial was to be found in Rotherhithe – a far cry from Eastbourne, but another haven for sailors. Here a new theatre opened a year later in October 1899 and was named the Terriss, a gesture which aligned him, however briefly, with that handful of actors commemorated in London's theatre directory. These included Garrick, Wyndham, and for a spell Seymour Hicks, so that two members of the family had their names singled out in this way in the decade following Terriss's death, though the Hicks became the Globe in 1909 and the Terriss changed its name to the Rotherhithe Hippodrome a year earlier.

In another sense Terriss may have forecast the duration of his fame more accurately than his admirers would allow. If so, it was the medium in which he shone, rather than his own limitations, which put a term to his fame. For any actor to achieve some measure of immortality he must have won success in a "classic" role. For English actors this is most commonly Shakespearean tragedy. Terriss was an acceptable Bassanio, Mercutio and Don Pedro, and a substantial Henry VIII. He was neither a Romeo nor an Othello, as his record in those roles emphasises. He was an unapproached David Kingsley, Jack Medway, and Dudley Keppel, but *Harbour Lights*, *The Union Jack*, and *One of the Best* stood no chance of surviving the revolution in entertainment which in the years following his death made the cinema, not the theatre, the medium of melodrama.

But the name of Terriss did survive that revolution. Ellaline and Seymour Hicks, rising courageously above the double disaster which had struck them, became the leading husband-and-wife team of Edwardian musical comedy. *A Runaway Girl*, which Seymour helped to write, opened less than six months after the catastrophe; *Bluebell in Fairyland* proved a recurrent favourite, and they achieved lasting and "legitimate" fame when they created Valentine Brown and Phoebe Throssel in Barrie's *Quality Street*. For the next forty years they were welcomed by audiences throughout the English-speaking world. When maturity interposed, they turned from the musical stage to light comedy. *The Man in Dress Clothes* and later *Vintage Wine*, both of which Seymour wrote, proved unfailing attractions whenever and wherever they were revived. In 1935 Seymour was knighted. Four years earlier he had received the order of Chevalier of the Legion of Honour for his contribution to Anglo-French *entente*. He died in 1949 at the age of 78. Ellaline retained her love of life and the loyalty of her public for another twenty-two years, surviving the magnificent occasion of her 100th birthday in April 1971 by three months.

If William Terriss's fame in the theatre world withered, his name began to figure regularly in the world of the supernatural. It was perhaps predictable that a popular idol who had met such a violent end would prove attractive to the collectors of ghost stories, and the Adelphi itself was the obvious scene for such reappearances. "Strange tappings and rapping noises" in his and Jessie's dressing-rooms were reported; followed by the "strange behaviour of mechanically sound lifts" and the "overwhelming impression of someone being present in the deserted theatre at night". A particularly sensitive witness was the musical comedy star June, who in 1928 opened at the Adelphi in a revue, *Clowns in Clover*. While resting in her dressing-room between a matinee and evening performance she became aware of the couch vibrating, as though being kicked from underneath, followed by a tight grip on her arm, sufficient to raise weals. Other witnesses spoke of a green light manifesting itself on the stage late at night.[5]

A less predictable series of appearances has been reported at Covent Garden tube station where "A travelling inspector on the Piccadilly Line claims to have seen the ghost at least forty times."[6] The figure appears late at night, after the last train has gone, and has been identified by "his old-fashioned clothes" and in particular pale gloves, which Terriss is said to have worn. At least one witness, a station foreman, Mr Jack Haydon, when shown Terriss's picture, confirmed the identification, and claimed to have seen the ghost "nearly every day in some part of the station for some two years". Other members of London Transport staff are less approachable. Electricians, who generally work at night in tube stations, have been forbidden to do so at Covent Garden "in case the ghost interferes with their potentially dangerous work", and a lady employee, after one manifestation, asked for an immediate transfer.[7]

In explanation of the ghost's preference for Covent Garden, it has been asserted that Terriss "used the station nightly to get from his Putney home to the theatre".[8] But the Piccadilly Line was not built until 1906, and the only route from Bedford Park open to the actor was the District Line via Turnham Green to Charing Cross. No doubt supernatural figures are not subject to the exigencies of London Transport timetables.

On Terriss's leading lady the delayed shock of his murder was understandably grievous. Bravely as Jessie had borne up during the funeral, she later suffered almost total collapse. With good friends to support her, she travelled to Italy and gradually found peace of mind in Venice, Florence and Rome. When she returned she vowed never to act again, but an offer from Charles Frohman, doubtless prompted by colleagues in London, was pressed on her by Irving and others. "While we live, we must work", he insisted, and eventually she agreed to accept a five-year contract.[9] Almost exactly a year after the tragedy at the Adelphi she opened at the Empire Theatre, New York, in an adaptation of Anthony Hope's novel, *Phroso*. During the next fifteen years she appeared almost exclusively in America, developing in middle age a vein of comedy she had had no chance of displaying at the Adelphi, and playing such parts as Lady Algernon Chetland in *Lord and Lady Algy*, Lady Eastney in *Mrs. Dane's Defence*, and even Beatrice in *Much Ado*.

It was also in New York in 1907 that she married the Scots actor John Glendinning, then appearing with her in Henry Arthur Jones's play, *The Hypocrites*. He had been working in America for over twenty years, but as a young man had toured the United Kingdom in Adelphi melodrama, often billed as "the Terriss of the North". There was consequently a double significance in this happy outcome to her years of loneliness, though that happiness was cut short in 1916 when her husband died at the age of fifty-eight. Jessie had retired in 1913, and ten years later published *Myself and Others*, written in collaboration with the journalist J. B. Booth. She lived until 1932.

But the murderer of William Terriss survived all the other leading figures in the drama. Richard Archer Prince was transferred to Broadmoor where he remained for forty years, dying in 1937. Despite his life sentence a belief persisted that he was at liberty and haunting the London theatre world. Edward Stirling, an actor-manager who ran an English company in Paris in the 1920s, relates that while auditioning in London he was approached by

> a grim-looking elderly man with an impressive list of past work. He appeared to have played in a great many excellent productions, but I felt unaccountably reluctant to engage him. However, as there was not much time, I asked him to come and read the part that afternoon.

After he had gone, a colleague exclaimed:

> "For God's sake don't say you've engaged that man!"
> "I haven't yet, but I almost certainly shall."
> "You can't."
> "Why not?"
> "That's the man who murdered Bill Terriss."

– and Stirling adds a footnote to explain that Prince had been "ultimately discharged" from Broadmoor.[10]

Others, more closely associated with the tragedy, sought reassurance. Tom Terriss records such an occasion:

> Some years later, Tom visited the asylum where his father's assassin was confined. The superintendent there told him that the demented man was in constant terror; that if Tom had any thoughts of vengeance, to give them up, for the man was being more than punished – his screams often woke the attendants in the middle of the night. The man thought he was being pursued by someone with a knife.[11]

Jessie Millward gives a contrary impression. Shortly before she published her autobiography, "an ex-Cabinet Minister" told her of a visit to Broadmoor:

> In the visitor's honour a performance was given by the asylum band, the members of which were prisoners found insane. The conductor mounted to his desk, turned to the ex-Minister and gave him a majestic bow, then, tapping on his desk in manner of the professional *chef d'orchestre*, proceeded to conduct the performance.
> That conductor was Prince, the murderer of my friend.[12]

It should be noted that the records of the hospital afford no support, either for these assertions or for the claim in the radio play, *A Study in Hatred*, broadcast in 1985, that Prince persuaded the authorities to allow him and his fellow-patients to stage a production of *Secret Service*, so that he could play the role in which Terriss had made his last appearance.

The final years of William Abingdon, the mysterious "other man" in the drama, are somewhat better documented. His timely move to the United States proved initially profitable. In 1906 he married a well-known American actress, Bijou Fernandez, who as a child had played Prince Arthur to Edwin Booth's King John. More importantly for Abingdon's career, her mother was a leading theatrical agent, and for some years her son-in-law found regular employment. But gradually the parts grew scarce and ultimately the marriage broke up. On 19 May 1918 Abingdon was found dead in his apartment at 235 West 76th Street, New York. He had cut his throat.

The newspaper accounts refer to longstanding depression and to anxiety over his two sons by a previous marriage, both then on active service in Europe. But a paragraph in a South African trade paper three months later adds some curious if unsubstantiated detail:

> In a small booklet upon which was engraved "*In memoriam* to William Terriss", Mr. Abingdon left this note: "For some time I have suffered from Neurasthenia, acute melancholia, a desire to avoid anything and everything. Insomnia. Just weary. Haven't been to the club in three weeks. Hiding away in cheap moving-picture shows, or staying in the house. Even baseball doesn't interest me. Everybody is against me, so one more mistake and then the great conundrum."[13]

Such particulars, supplemented by the comment:

> In Mr. Abingdon's diary for the six days before his suicide he had drawn a question mark opposite the date. He wrote in his diary one single word, which he had been called on to use thousands of times in his career upon the stage. It was "Exit".

suggest a conveniently fruitful imagination at work. How did a Johannesburg journalist have sight of a document not mentioned in any of the American accounts of Abingdon's death? It should, however, be added that the paragraph also states: "William Terriss was another English actor of Mr. Abingdon's school. It will be remembered that he was murdered in London in 1897. The two players had been life-long friends." Any published connection between Abingdon and Terriss's murder dates from Seymour Hicks's veiled reference to a "Mr. A." in 1930. If the South African's story was invented, he showed extraordinary insight.

Adelphi melodrama itself did not long survive its most popular interpreter. A desperate attempt to resume the run of *Secret Service*, with Herbert Waring and May Whitty in Terriss's and Jessie's roles, lasted only a couple of weeks. As a result the Gattis were content to let the theatre to outside managements, and in 1901 the name was changed to the Century Theatre, perhaps to exorcise the associations of the past few years. If so, the public objected, and the name Adelphi was restored the following year. Henceforward the theatre would house not melodrama but chiefly musical comedy. There were brief periods when the management aspired higher, notably a spell of Shakespeare and new verse drama under Oscar Asche and Lily Brayton between 1904 and 1906, but the cheerful strains of the Edwardian musical play proved its salvation. At the same time the Lyceum, once the Adelphi's superior, fell on difficult days. It never recovered its identity after Irving left in 1902, operated briefly as a music hall, and was then associated with the sensational brand of melodrama purveyed by the Melville Brothers. Indeed the Strand as a theatrical highway suffered increasing competition from the growing number of theatres arising along the newly opened Shaftesbury Avenue. It survived the challenge, but there would never be another Irving to bring his extraordinary blend of mystery and magic to the Lyceum, or another Terriss to fill the Adelphi with his unique appeal. They were both irreplaceable.

The active life of a leading actor must by its very nature end well before his death. Like most performers his pre-eminence derives from personal attributes and physical powers exhibited at their peak, and in this respect his career more closely resembles that of an athlete than of an artist, whose work survives to be judged and admired. Once the actor's powers wane, the theatre has little use for him. Even his experience and wisdom can find few outlets, for (unlike the political or industrial arena) the theatrical profession is not organised to benefit from the counsels of yesterday's leaders.

This is especially true of the nineteenth-century theatre, with its precarious finances and cut-throat competition. In an age before the cinema and television offered wider fame and richer rewards, the stage devoured its favourites and cast them aside. Provident actors retired early: Macready, for instance, left the stage at fifty-seven; Squire Bancroft at forty-four, though both lived to see old age. The improvident found themselves working less and less, further from the limelight, often "supporting" in some humble capacity their triumphant successors. Even those who died young were frequently already burnt out; Edmund Kean, for example, was already a spent force when he died at forty-four.

In falling to the assassin's knife William Terriss escaped this fate. He died at the height of his fame, still possessing the looks and physique of the romantic hero, still idolised by a vast public on both sides of the Atlantic. There was no final chapter in his career such as darkened the last days of his former "Guv'nor", Henry Irving, when, deposed from his throne at the Lyceum, he struggled through the provinces with failing health and fading fortunes to keep his creditors satisfied. Terriss died as he had lived, the hero of the play in which he was appearing and the star of the theatre in which he was struck down.

Moreover, tragically premature as his end seemed to his contemporaries, there was a certain appropriateness artistically about its timing, both as regards his own prospects at the age of fifty, and more particularly the prospects of the drama itself. For by 1897 romantic melodrama, to which much of his career had been devoted, faced a growing threat from the moving picture. The cinema, although still silent, would encompass most of the effects in which the theatre had chiefly traded during the preceding century: spectacle, movement, pathos, patriotism. The cinema could also offer its wares simultaneously throughout the world, conferring on its earliest favourites a fame such as Garrick or Kean never enjoyed or even envisaged. Not for Terriss, therefore, the invidious comparisons between a stage-hero past his prime and the rising star of a Valentino or Douglas Fairbanks.

This account has turned repeatedly to Ellen Terry for a vivid portrait in words or an apt comment. Her judgment on the death of a close colleague and intimate friend is unchallengeable:

He died as a beautiful youth, a kind of Adonis, although he was fifty years old.[14]

and her son echoes her:

Terriss was very fond of that motto, "Carpe Diem", and ended one of his letters: *"and in the dim future give a few thoughts to old Carpe Diem."*
I have given many a thought to him since he died in 1897, but always the thoughts resolved themselves into remembrances of a *young* "Carpe Diem".[15]

He deserves to be remembered still.

Notes

1 I am indebted to Robert Stuart for permission to quote from this source.
2 *Henry Irving* p. 106.
3 January 1898.
4 *Times* 17 July 1898.
5 Peter Underwood: *Haunted London* (London, Harrap, 1973) pp. 41–3.
6 Jack Hallam: *Ghosts of London* (London, Wolfe Publishing Company, 1975) pp. 57–8.
7 W. B. Herbert: *Railway Ghosts* (Newton Abbott, David and Charles, 1985) pp. 92–4.
8 Hallam: *Ghosts of London* p. 58
9 Millward p. 243.
10 W. Edward Stirling: *Something to Declare* (London, Frederick Muller, 1942) p. 62.
11 Chapter X p. 4.
12 Millward: pp. 237–8.
13 *Stage, Screen and South African Pictorial*, Johannesburg, 17 August 1918, p. 4. I am indebted to Professor Robert Lawrence for drawing this item to my attention.
14 Terry p. 113.
15 *Henry Irving* p. 107.

Bibliography

Manuscript sources

Scrapbook of Cuttings, Photographs, Letters and other material assembled by Harriet Lewin (Terriss's sister) and kindly made available to me by Mr. Robert Stuart (Terriss's great-grandson).

Typescript of "Projected Autobiography of Tom Terriss" written with Christy Squire (Chapters I–V completed; Chapters VI–XXXIV in synopsis) kindly made available to me by Mr. Robert Stuart.

Letters in the Harvard University Theatre Collection.

Newspapers Etc.

Times, London.
Era, London.
Stage, London.
Theatre, London, particularly "'William Terriss' by an Old Playgoer".
   NS Vol. VI 1 December 1882, pp. 332–337.
   "Stars of the Stage No. 1: Mr. William Terriss" by Hartley Aspden.
   NS Vol. XXI 1 May 1893 pp. 243–254.
Dundee Advertiser, Dundee Courier, Dundee People's Journal, December 1897 – January 1898 for the background to Richard Archer (Prince) and the Archer family.

Books

Squire and Marie Bancroft. *Mr. and Mrs. Bancroft: On and Off the Stage.* (London, Bentley, 1889)
Madeleine Bingham. *Henry Irving and the Victorian Theatre.* (London, Allen & Unwin, 1978)

Michael R. Booth. *English Melodrama*. (London, Herbert Jenkins, 1965)

Jean Webster Brough. *Prompt Copy: The Brough Story*. (London, Hutchinson, 1952)

Edward Gordon Craig. *Henry Irving*. (London, Dent, 1930)

Beatrice Forbes-Robertson. *Family Legend*. (Privately printed, 1973)

Johnston Forbes-Robertson. *A Player under Three Reigns* (London, Fisher Unwin, 1925)

Jack Hallam. *Ghosts of London*. (London, Wolfe Publishing Company, 1975)

W. B. Herbert. *Railway Ghosts*. (Newton Abbott, David & Charles, 1985)

Seymour Hicks. *Between Ourselves*. (London, Cassell, 1930)

Laurence Irving. *Henry Irving: The Actor and His World*. (London, Faber, 1951)

Jerome K. Jerome. *Stage-Land: Curious Habits and Customs of its Inhabitants* (London, Chatto & Windus, 1889)

Jessie Millward (in collaboration with J. B. Booth). *Myself and Others*. (London, Hutchinson, 1923)

W. Graham Robertson. *Time Was*. (London, Hamish Hamilton, 1931)

George Rowell. *Queen Victoria Goes to the Theatre*. (London, Paul Elek, 1978)

Theatre in the Age of Irving. (Oxford, Blackwell, 1981)

The Victorian Theatre 1792–1914: A Survey. (Cambridge, Cambridge University Press, 1978)

"Mercutio as Romeo: William Terriss in *Romeo and Juliet*" in Richard Foulkes (Editor). *Shakespeare and the Victorian Stage*. (Cambridge, Cambridge University Press, 1986)

H. A. Saintsbury and Cecil Palmer (Editors). *We Saw Him Act*. (London, Hurst & Blackett, 1939)

George R. Sims. *My Life*. (London, Eveleigh Nash, 1917)

Arthur J. Smythe. *The Life of William Terriss, Actor*. (London, Archibald Constable, 1898)

Edward Stirling. *Something to Declare* (London, Frederick Muller, 1942)

Christopher St. John (Editor). *Ellen Terry and Bernard Shaw: A Correspondence*. (London, Reinhardt & Evans, 1949)

Ellaline Terriss. *Just a Little Bit of String*. (London, Hutchinson, 1955)

Ellen Terry. *Ellen Terry's Memoirs*, with notes by Edith Craig and Christopher St. John. (London, Gollancz, 1933)

Peter Underwood. *Haunted London*. (London, Harrap, 1973)

Index

Index

Index

Index

Index